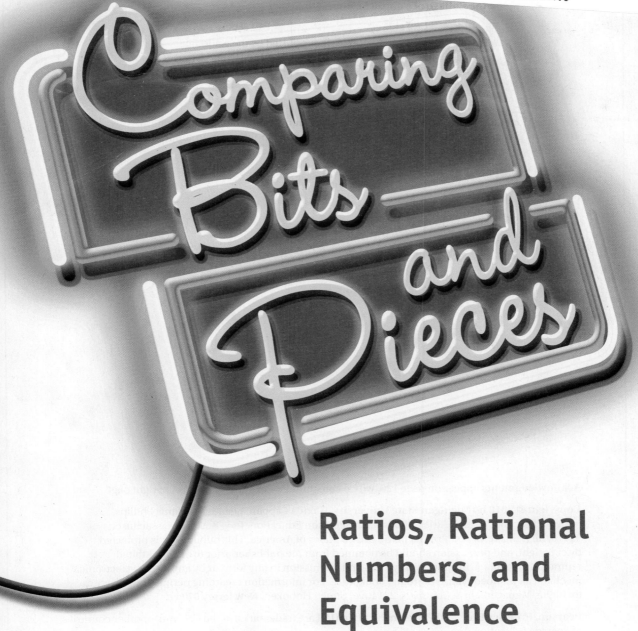

Comparing Bits and Pieces

Ratios, Rational Numbers, and Equivalence

Glenda Lappan, Elizabeth Difanis Phillips,
James T. Fey, Susan N. Friel

Pearson

Boston, Massachusetts

Connected Mathematics® was developed at Michigan State University with financial support from the Michigan State University Office of the Provost, Computing and Technology, and the College of Natural Science.

This material is based upon work supported by the National Science Foundation under Grant No. MDR 9150217 and Grant No. ESI 9986372. Opinions expressed are those of the authors and not necessarily those of the Foundation.

As with prior editions of this work, the authors and administration of Michigan State University preserve a tradition of devoting royalties from this publication to support activities sponsored by the MSU Mathematics Education Enrichment Fund.

13-digit ISBN 978-0-328-90039-8
10-digit ISBN 0-328-90039-7

2 17

A Team of Experts

Glenda Lappan is a University Distinguished Professor in the Program in Mathematics Education (PRIME) and the Department of Mathematics at Michigan State University. Her research and development interests are in the connected areas of students' learning of mathematics and mathematics teachers' professional growth and change related to the development and enactment of K–12 curriculum materials.

Elizabeth Difanis Phillips is a Senior Academic Specialist in the Program in Mathematics Education (PRIME) and the Department of Mathematics at Michigan State University. She is interested in teaching and learning mathematics for both teachers and students. These interests have led to curriculum and professional development projects at the middle school and high school levels, as well as projects related to the teaching and learning of algebra across the grades.

James T. Fey is a Professor Emeritus at the University of Maryland. His consistent professional interest has been development and research focused on curriculum materials that engage middle and high school students in problem-based collaborative investigations of mathematical ideas and their applications.

Susan N. Friel is a Professor of Mathematics Education in the School of Education at the University of North Carolina at Chapel Hill. Her research interests focus on statistics education for middle-grade students and, more broadly, on teachers' professional development and growth in teaching mathematics K–8.

With... Yvonne Grant and Jacqueline Stewart

Yvonne Grant teaches mathematics at Portland Middle School in Portland, Michigan. Jacqueline Stewart is a recently retired high school teacher of mathematics at Okemos High School in Okemos, Michigan. Both Yvonne and Jacqueline have worked on a variety of activities related to the development, implementation, and professional development of the CMP curriculum since its beginning in 1991.

Development Team

CMP3 Authors

Glenda Lappan, University Distinguished Professor, Michigan State University
Elizabeth Difanis Phillips, Senior Academic Specialist, Michigan State University
James T. Fey, Professor Emeritus, University of Maryland
Susan N. Friel, Professor, University of North Carolina – Chapel Hill

With...

Yvonne Grant, Portland Middle School, Michigan
Jacqueline Stewart, Mathematics Consultant, Mason, Michigan

In Memory of... William M. Fitzgerald, Professor (Deceased), Michigan State University, who made substantial contributions to conceptualizing and creating CMP1.

Administrative Assistant

Michigan State University
Judith Martus Miller

Support Staff

Michigan State University
Undergraduate Assistants:
Bradley Robert Corlett, Carly Fleming, Erin Lucian, Scooter Nowak

Development Assistants

Michigan State University
Graduate Research Assistants:
Richard "Abe" Edwards, Nic Gilbertson, Funda Gonulates, Aladar Horvath, Eun Mi Kim, Kevin Lawrence, Jennifer Nimtz, Joanne Philhower, Sasha Wang

Assessment Team

Maine
Falmouth Public Schools
Falmouth Middle School: Shawn Towle

Michigan
Ann Arbor Public Schools
Tappan Middle School
Anne Marie Nicoll-Turner

Portland Public Schools
Portland Middle School
Holly DeRosia, Yvonne Grant

Traverse City Area Public Schools
Traverse City East Middle School
Jane Porath, Mary Beth Schmitt

Traverse City West Middle School
Jennifer Rundio, Karrie Tufts

Ohio
Clark-Shawnee Local Schools
Rockway Middle School: Jim Mamer

Content Consultants

Michigan State University
Peter Lappan, Professor Emeritus, Department of Mathematics

Normandale Community College
Christopher Danielson, Instructor, Department of Mathematics & Statistics

University of North Carolina – Wilmington
Dargan Frierson, Jr., Professor, Department of Mathematics & Statistics

Student Activities
Michigan State University
Brin Keller, Associate Professor, Department of Mathematics

Consultants

Indiana
Purdue University
Mary Bouck, Mathematics Consultant

Michigan
Oakland Schools
Valerie Mills, Mathematics Education
Supervisor
Mathematics Education Consultants:
Geraldine Devine, Dana Gosen

Ellen Bacon, Independent Mathematics
Consultant

New York
University of Rochester
Jeffrey Choppin, Associate Professor

Ohio
University of Toledo
Debra Johanning, Associate Professor

Pennsylvania
University of Pittsburgh
Margaret Smith, Professor

Texas
University of Texas at Austin
Emma Trevino, Supervisor of
Mathematics Programs, The Dana Center

Mathematics for All Consulting
Carmen Whitman, Mathematics Consultant

....

Reviewers

Michigan
Ionia Public Schools
Kathy Dole, Director of Curriculum
and Instruction

Grand Valley State University
Lisa Kasmer, Assistant Professor

Portland Public Schools
Teri Keusch, Classroom Teacher

Minnesota
Hopkins School District 270
Michele Luke, Mathematics Coordinator

....

Field Test Sites for CMP3

Michigan
Ann Arbor Public Schools
Tappan Middle School
Anne Marie Nicoll-Turner*

Portland Public Schools
Portland Middle School: Mark Braun,
Angela Buckland, Holly DeRosia,
Holly Feldpausch, Angela Foote,
Yvonne Grant*, Kristin Roberts,
Angie Stump, Tammi Wardwell

Traverse City Area Public Schools
Traverse City East Middle School
Ivanka Baic Berkshire, Brenda Dunscombe,
Tracie Herzberg, Deb Larimer, Jan Palkowski,
Rebecca Perreault, Jane Porath*,
Robert Sagan, Mary Beth Schmitt*

Traverse City West Middle School
Pamela Alfieri, Jennifer Rundio,
Maria Taplin, Karrie Tufts*

Maine
Falmouth Public Schools
Falmouth Middle School: Sally Bennett,
Chris Driscoll, Sara Jones, Shawn Towle*

Minnesota
Minneapolis Public Schools
Jefferson Community School
Leif Carlson*,
Katrina Hayek Munsisoumang*

Ohio
Clark-Shawnee Local Schools
Reid School: Joanne Gilley
Rockway Middle School: Jim Mamer*
Possum School: Tami Thomas

*Indicates a Field Test Site Coordinator

Ratios, Rational Numbers, and Equivalence

Looking Ahead

The juice dispenser holds 120 cups of juice. About **what** fraction of the dispenser is filled with juice? About how many more cups of juice would it take to fill the dispenser?

Griffin visited her grandfather in Canada twice in the same year. Griffin says the absolute value of the temperature each day was 10. **What** could be the difference between the two temperatures in degrees?

A survey asked people about their physical characteristics. Out of the 30 people surveyed, 7 people reported having curly hair. **What** percent of the people surveyed have curly hair?

Sometimes whole numbers cannot communicate needed information precisely. You may need to talk about parts of wholes: "What fraction of the students going on this field trip are eighth-graders?" You may also need ways to discuss how to share, divide, or measure things: "What part of the pizza will each person get?" or "How tall are you?" Fractions, decimals, and percents are all ways of expressing quantities or measures.

There are many situations in which you may want to compare numbers. Comparing by subtracting is one way: "I have $2.00 more than my sister." Comparing with ratios gives different information: "I have twice as much money as my sister." Many comparisons in the real world are based on ratios rather than on differences.

In *Comparing Bits and Pieces,* you will develop skills with fractions, decimals, ratios and percents. Your new skills can help you make sense of situations like the ones on the previous page.

Mathematical Highlights

Comparing Bits and Pieces

In *Comparing Bits and Pieces,* you will develop your skills in using fractions, decimals, ratios and percents to measure and to compare quantities.

The Investigations in this Unit will help you understand how to:

- Use ratio language and notation to compare quantities
- Distinguish between fractions as numbers and ratios as comparisons
- Use a variety of scaling and partitioning strategies to reason proportionally
- Think of fractions and decimals as both locations and distances on the number line
- Move flexibly among fraction, decimal, and percent representations
- Find absolute values and opposites, and use them to describe real-world quantities
- Use fraction, decimal, and percent benchmarks to estimate numbers
- Use context, models, drawings, or estimation to reason about situations
- Use equivalence of fractions and ratios to solve problems
- Use rate tables and unit rates to solve problems

As you work on the problems in this Unit, ask yourself questions about situations that involve fractions, decimals, ratios and percents.

What models or diagrams might be helpful in understanding the situation and the relationships among quantities?

Is this a comparison situation? If so, do I use ratios or subtraction?

What strategies can I use to find equivalent forms of these fractions, decimals, ratios, or percents?

What strategies can I use to compare or order a set of fractions, decimals, and percents?

What strategies can I use to reason about numbers greater than or less than 0?

How can I use unit rates or rate table to make comparisons?

Mathematical Practices and Habits of Mind

In the *Connected Mathematics* curriculum you will develop an understanding of important mathematical ideas by solving problems and reflecting on the mathematics involved. Every day, you will use "habits of mind" to make sense of problems and apply what you learn to new situations. Some of these habits are described by the *Common Core State Standards for Mathematical Practices* (MP).

MP1 Make sense of problems and persevere in solving them.

When using mathematics to solve a problem, it helps to think carefully about

- data and other facts you are given and what additional information you need to solve the problem;

- strategies you have used to solve similar problems and whether you could solve a related simpler problem first;

- how you could express the problem with equations, diagrams, or graphs;

- whether your answer makes sense.

MP2 Reason abstractly and quantitatively.

When you are asked to solve a problem, it often helps to

- focus first on the key mathematical ideas;

- check that your answer makes sense in the problem setting;

- use what you know about the problem setting to guide your mathematical reasoning.

MP3 Construct viable arguments and critique the reasoning of others.

When you are asked to explain why a conjecture is correct, you can

- show some examples that fit the claim and explain why they fit;

- show how a new result follows logically from known facts and principles.

When you believe a mathematical claim is incorrect, you can

- show one or more counterexamples—cases that don't fit the claim;

- find steps in the argument that do not follow logically from prior claims.

MP4 Model with mathematics.

When you are asked to solve problems, it often helps to

- think carefully about the numbers or geometric shapes that are the most important factors in the problem, then ask yourself how those factors are related to each other;
- express data and relationships in the problem with tables, graphs, diagrams, or equations, and check your result to see if it makes sense.

MP5 Use appropriate tools strategically.

When working on mathematical questions, you should always

- decide which tools are most helpful for solving the problem and why;
- try a different tool when you get stuck.

MP6 Attend to precision.

In every mathematical exploration or problem-solving task, it is important to

- think carefully about the required accuracy of results; is a number estimate or geometric sketch good enough, or is a precise value or drawing needed?
- report your discoveries with clear and correct mathematical language that can be understood by those to whom you are speaking or writing.

MP7 Look for and make use of structure.

In mathematical explorations and problem solving, it is often helpful to

- look for patterns that show how data points, numbers, or geometric shapes are related to each other;
- use patterns to make predictions.

MP8 Look for and express regularity in repeated reasoning.

When results of a repeated calculation show a pattern, it helps to

- express that pattern as a general rule that can be used in similar cases;
- look for shortcuts that will make the calculation simpler in other cases.

You will use all of the Mathematical Practices in this Unit. Sometimes, when you look at a Problem, it is obvious which practice is most helpful. At other times, you will decide on a practice to use during class explorations and discussions. After completing each Problem, ask yourself:

- What mathematics have I learned by solving this Problem?
- What Mathematical Practices were helpful in learning this mathematics?

Making Comparisons

People make and do amazing and amusing things all over the world. For instance, the smallest motorized car is so small it has a bumper $\frac{1}{2}$ the thickness of a human hair, and its top speed is 0.011 miles per hour. It's so small it can sit on a fingernail!

On the next page are some more statements about people, places, and things. Notice that numbers are at the heart of each of these claims.

Common Core State Standards

6.RP.A.1 Understand the concept of a ratio and use ratio language to describe a ratio relationship between two quantities.

6.RP.A.3 Use ratio and rate reasoning to solve real-world and mathematical problems, e.g., by reasoning about tables of equivalent ratios, tape diagrams, double number line diagrams, or equations.

6.NS.C.6 Understand a rational number as a point on the number line . . .

Also 6.RP.A.2 and 6.NS.B.4

- The longest plunge over the edge of a waterfall in a kayak by a woman is 82 feet.

- The region of the world with the most biodiversity is the Tropical Andes of South America, where approximately 16% of all known plant species live.

- The winner of the first official backward running race ran one mile in 6 minutes 2.35 seconds.

Many world records use numbers that tell *how many* or *how much*. To make sense of number claims you need understanding and skill in using whole numbers, fractions, decimals, and percents to count, measure, and compare quantities. The goal of this Unit is to extend your ability to use fractions, decimals, percents, and ratios to solve problems, and to explain, compare, or quantify happenings in the world.

1.1 Fundraising
Comparing With Fractions and Ratios

Students at a middle school are organizing three fundraising projects to raise money. The eighth grade will sell calendars. The seventh grade will sell popcorn. The sixth grade will sell posters.

Each grade picks a different goal for its fundraiser. The three grades are competing to see which grade will reach its fundraising goal first.

The fundraising goal for each grade is displayed on a banner in front of the principal's office.

Fundraising Goals

6th grade	7th grade	8th grade
$ 300	$ 450	$ 150

- How can you compare the grades' fundraising goals?

Problem 1.1

A The students wrote some claims about the fundraising goals on slips of paper and gave them to the principal to read over the loudspeaker during the morning announcements. Decide whether each claim is true. Explain your reasoning.

> **Markus:**
> The sixth-grade goal is $150 more than the eighth-grade goal.

> **Kimi:**
> When the sixth graders meet their goal, they will have raised $\frac{2}{3}$ of the seventh-grade goal.

> **Lakisha:**
> The eighth-grade goal is half the sixth-grade goal.

> **Andres:**
> For every dollar the eighth graders plan to raise, the sixth graders plan to raise two dollars.

> **Ben:**
> For every $60 the sixth graders plan to raise, the seventh graders plan to raise $90.

> **Eliza:**
> The sixth-grade goal is 200% of the eighth-grade goal.

> **Chung:**
> For every $3 the eighth grade plans to raise, the seventh grade plans to raise $1.

Problem **1.1** *continued*

B Write three more true comparison statements for the principal to read over the loudspeaker.

C On the first day of the fundraiser, the principal announces one more goal over the loudspeaker—the teachers' fundraising goal. The microphone is not working very well. What do you think the teachers' goal is?

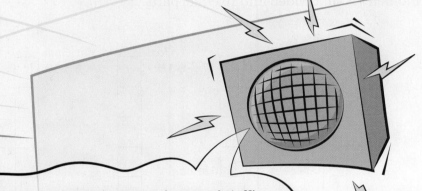

Good morning students, teachers, and staff!
The teachers have joined the school fundraiser.
They will be selling books for summer reading.
They have set a goal of STATIC dollars.

This is 210 dollars more than the STATIC graders,
but only $\frac{4}{5}$ as much as the STATIC graders.
For every 60 dollars the teachers plan to raise,
the STATIC graders plan to raise 50 dollars.

A C E Homework starts on page 27.

1.2 Fundraising Thermometers
Introducing Ratios

The principal at the middle school shows each grade's fundraising progress on charts that look like thermometers. The principal records the progress shown on the thermometer using fractions and dollar amounts. The fundraiser lasts 10 days. Each day, the principal announces the progress of each grade over the loudspeaker.

The thermometers are all the same length, despite the different goals. Each thermometer is subdivided into 10 equal parts.

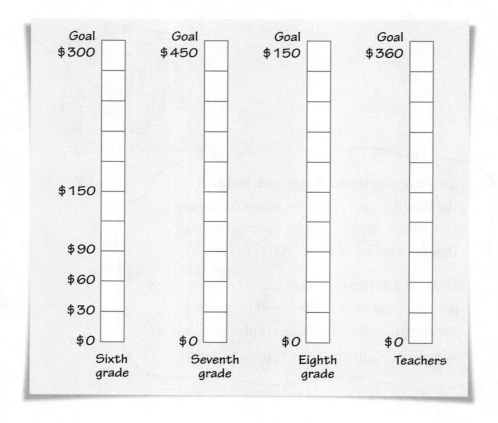

- How can you use the thermometers to make comparisons among the goals?

Comparing Bits and Pieces

Problem 1.2

Ⓐ The principal labeled some of the marks on the four thermometers with dollar amounts. Decide what labels belong on the remaining marks.

Ⓑ **1.** Ben said: *For every $60 the sixth graders plan to raise, the seventh graders plan to raise $90.* He looks at the principal's thermometers and sees that $60 is at the same place on the sixth-grade thermometer as $90 is on the seventh-grade thermometer.

Ben also makes the claim: *For every $30 the sixth graders plan to raise, the seventh graders plan to raise $45.*

Do you agree with this claim? Explain your reasoning.

2. Use the thermometers to write two more *for every* claims that relate the fundraising goals.

Ⓒ You can write each of the comparisons in Question B as a *ratio*. A **ratio** is a kind of comparison.

Here are two ways that you can rewrite the comparisons in Question B.

The ratio of the sixth-grade goal to the seventh-grade goal is 60 to 90.

The ratio of the sixth-grade goal to the seventh-grade goal is 30 to 45.

1. What do the numbers 60, 90, 30, and 45 mean in each ratio statement?

2. Rewrite your comparisons from Question B part 2 using the word *ratio*.

Ⓓ **1.** The ratios from Ben's statements show the same relationship using different numbers. These ratios are *equivalent*. List some other pairs of equivalent ratios you have found in this Problem.

2. What patterns do you notice in your ratios that can help you find other equivalent ratios?

ⒶⒸⒺ Homework starts on page 27.

1.3 On the Line
Equivalent Fractions and the Number Line

The sixth graders made their own fundraising thermometer to record their progress. At the end of each day, they compare the total amount they have raised to their goal. The shaded part of the thermometer represents the fraction of the goal the sixth graders have raised. Their challenge is to figure out how to represent dollar amounts as a fraction of $300. They make fraction strips to help them correctly shade their thermometer.

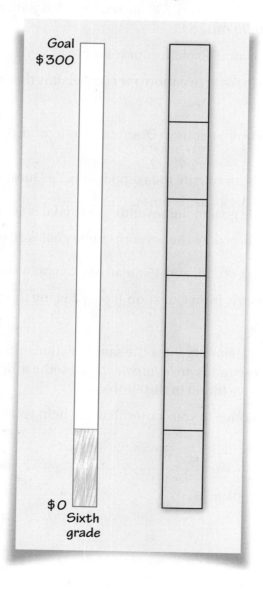

Goal
$300

$0
Sixth
grade

- Have the sixth graders collected more than $\frac{1}{10}$ of their goal? More than $\frac{2}{10}$?

- The thermometer shows the amount they raised on Day 1. What fraction of their goal have they raised?

In this Problem, you will fold fraction strips like those of the sixth graders so that you can measure each day's progress.

As you fold your strips, think about the strategies you use to make them and about the relationships between the size and number of parts on the various strips.

One important relationship to look for is when the marks on your fraction strips match up, even though the total number of parts on each strip is different. The places where marks match show **equivalent fractions.** Fractions that are equivalent represent the same amount even though their names are different.

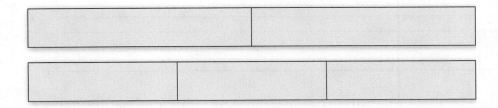

What equivalent fractions can you see with these two fraction strips?

- What relationships do you see among your fraction strips?
- What patterns do you see that will help you fold different fraction strips?

Problem 1.3

A **1.** Use strips of paper $8\frac{1}{2}$ inches long. Each strip represents 1 whole. Fold the strips to show halves, thirds, fourths, fifths, sixths, eighths, ninths, tenths, and twelfths. Mark the folds so you can see them easily, as shown below.

2. What strategies did you use to fold your strips?

B **1.** How can you use the halves strip to fold eighths?

2. The picture below shows a student's halves, fourths, and eighths strips. How does the size of one part of a halves strip compare to the size of one part of an eighths strip?

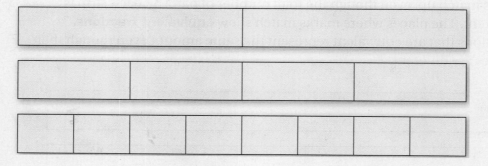

3. What fraction strips can you make if you start with a thirds strip?

4. Which of the fraction strips you folded have at least one mark that lines up with a mark on a twelfths strip? What equivalent fractions do the matching marks on the strips suggest?

Problem **1.3** continued

C In earlier grades, you used number lines, such as the one below, to show whole numbers.

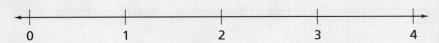

Now you can use fraction strips to mark points between whole numbers.

You start by using a fraction strip to mark and label 0 and 1 on a number line on your paper.

1. Some students began to make a number line using their one-third, one-sixth, one-ninth, and one-twelfth fraction strips. The drawing shows their work so far. One student used the top fraction strip to mark $\frac{2}{3}$ on the number line.

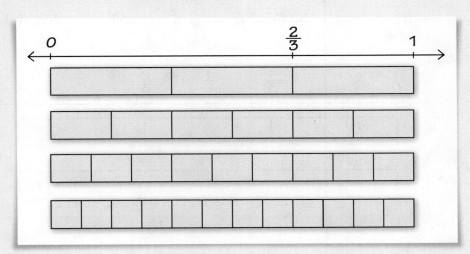

   a. Name three other fractions shown here that are equivalent to $\frac{2}{3}$.

   b. Name another fraction equivalent to $\frac{2}{3}$.

2. If you have used a fraction strip to name a specific point between 0 and 1 on a number line, how can you find equivalent fractions to name this point?

continued on the next page >

Problem **1.3** *continued*

D Some other students began to mark a number line using different fraction strips. Use their drawings to measure distances between points. For example, the distance between the mark labeled 0 and the mark labeled $\frac{3}{5}$ is $\frac{3}{5}$.

1.

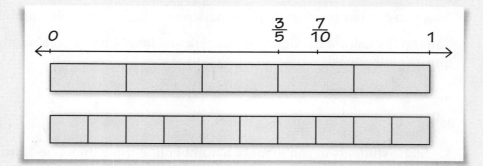

What is the distance between each pair of points?

a. 0 and $\frac{7}{10}$ **b.** $\frac{3}{5}$ and $\frac{7}{10}$ **c.** $\frac{7}{10}$ and 1   **d.** $\frac{3}{5}$ and 1

2.

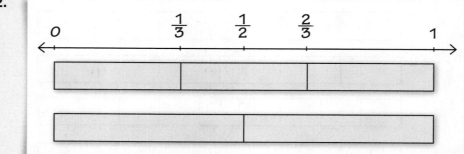

What is the distance between each pair of points?

a. 0 and $\frac{1}{3}$ **b.** $\frac{1}{3}$ and $\frac{1}{2}$ **c.** $\frac{1}{3}$ and $\frac{2}{3}$

d. $\frac{1}{2}$ and $\frac{2}{3}$ **e.** $\frac{1}{2}$ and 1   **f.** $\frac{2}{3}$ and 1

Problem **1.3** *continued*

E 1. Name five fractions equivalent to $\frac{4}{12}$.

2. Name five fractions that are near, but not equivalent to, $\frac{4}{12}$.

3. How can fraction strips, number lines, and thinking with numbers help you find equivalent fractions?

4. Matt claims that $\frac{1}{3}$ can indicate a point on a number line as well as distance. Is he correct? Explain.

5. Sally said that the fraction strips remind her of rulers and that you could use fraction strips to measure the progress on the fundraising thermometers. What do you think?

Save your fraction strips to use with Problem 1.4.

 Homework starts on page 27.

Did You Know?

Hieroglyphic inscriptions show that, with the exception of $\frac{2}{3}$, Egyptian mathematicians only used fractions with 1 in the numerator. These fractions, such as $\frac{1}{2}$ and $\frac{1}{16}$, are *unit fractions*. The Egyptians expressed other fractions as sums of unit fractions. For example, they expressed the fraction $\frac{5}{12}$ as $\frac{1}{4} + \frac{1}{6}$ (as shown in the second and third pieces of the hieroglyphics below).

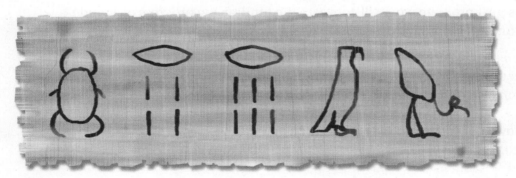

Check with fraction strips to see that $\frac{1}{4} + \frac{1}{6} = \frac{5}{12}$. You studied unit fractions in earlier grades. How do unit fractions appear on fraction strips? On a number line?

1.4 Measuring Progress
Finding Fractional Parts

Here are two claims about the fundraising goals from Problem 1.1.

> **Ben:**
>
> For every $60 the sixth graders plan to raise,
> the seventh graders plan to raise $90.

> **Kimi:**
>
> When the sixth graders meet their goal, they will
> have raised $\frac{2}{3}$ of the seventh-grade goal.

Ben and Kimi are each comparing one sixth-grade goal to one seventh-grade goal. Ben uses ratios to make comparisons and Kimi uses fractions to make comparisons.

- Think about some ways in which working with fractions is like and not like working with ratios.

When you use fractions to compare a part to a whole, you often have more than one fraction name for the same quantity. For example, in Problem 1.3, you found that $\frac{1}{5} = \frac{2}{10}$.

In this next problem, you will compare the fundraising progress of a grade to its fundraising goal using fractions.

The thermometers on the next page show the progress of the sixth-grade poster sales after 2, 4, 6, 8, and 10 days. The principal needs to know what fraction of the goal the sixth grade has achieved after each day.

- How can you use your fraction strips to measure the sixth-grade's progress?

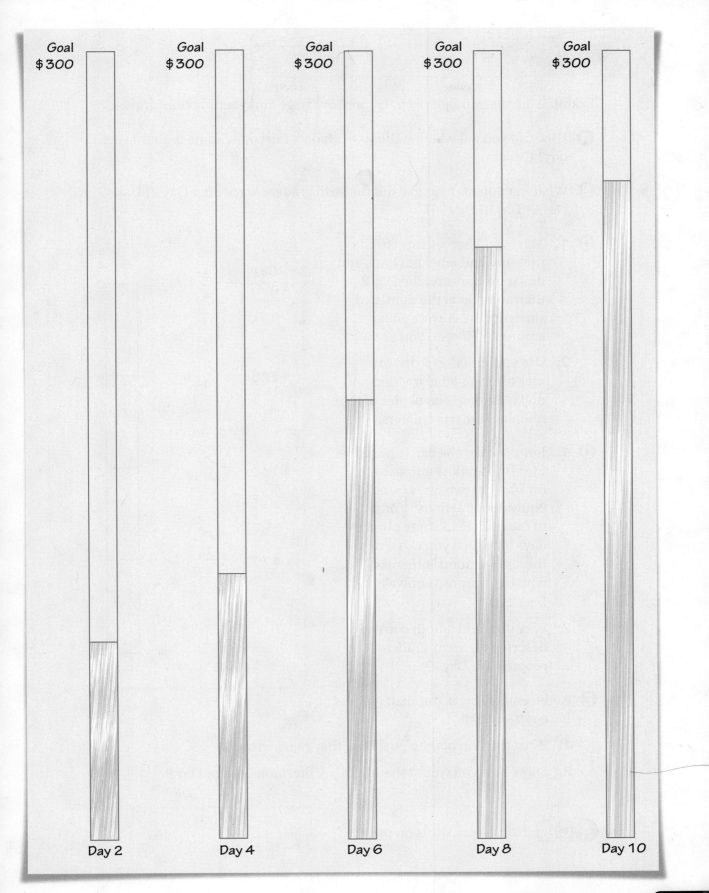

Problem 1.4

Examine the thermometers on the previous page and your fraction strips.

A How can you tell whether the sixth graders raised the same amount each day? Explain.

B What fraction of their goal did the sixth graders reach after Day 2? Day 4? Day 6? Day 8? Day 10?

C **1.** Mary used her fourths strip to measure and label fractions and dollar amounts on the Day 2 thermometer at the right. Did she write the correct dollar amounts? How do you know?

   2. Use your fraction strips to measure and label fraction and dollar amounts on copies of the remaining thermometers.

D **1.** Jeri says that she can express the sixth-graders' progress on Day 2 in two ways using equivalent fractions: $\frac{1}{4}$ or $\frac{2}{8}$ of the goal. Find some other days for which you can write the sixth-graders' progress with two or more equivalent fractions.

   2. Why do $\frac{1}{4}$ and $\frac{2}{8}$ both correctly describe the sixth-graders' progress on Day 2?

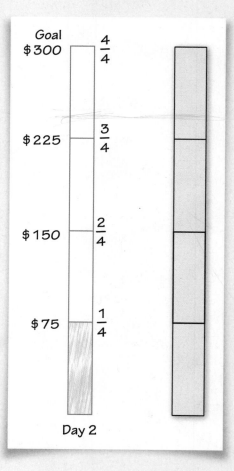

Day 2

E At the end of Day 9, the sixth graders have raised $240.

   1. What fraction of their goal have they reached?

   2. Show how you would shade a blank thermometer for Day 9.

 Homework starts on page 27.

1.5 Comparing Fundraising Goals
Using Fractions and Ratios

In Problem 1.4, you used fractions to find parts of the sixth-graders' fundraising goal. Fraction strips and pictures such as fundraising thermometers are sometimes called **tape diagrams.** This is because a fraction strip is a long, skinny rectangle, like a long piece of tape.

In this Problem, you will use fractions to find parts of the other goals, and you will use ratios to compare the amounts raised by different grades.

A ratio comparison statement uses both numbers and words to show how two quantities are related. To write ratios, you can use the words *for every*, *to*, or a colon (:). For example, you may write these comparison statements.

For every $60 dollars the sixth graders raise, the seventh graders raise $90.

or

The ratio of the sixth-grade goal to the seventh-grade goal is 60 to 90.

or

The ratio of the sixth-grade goal to the seventh-grade goal is 60 : 90.

You read the colon ":" using the word *to*. Both the word *to* and the colon are common in mathematics.

The fundraising thermometers on the next page show the goals and the progress of each grade and of the teachers after ten days.

- Which situations involve fractions? Ratios? How can you decide?

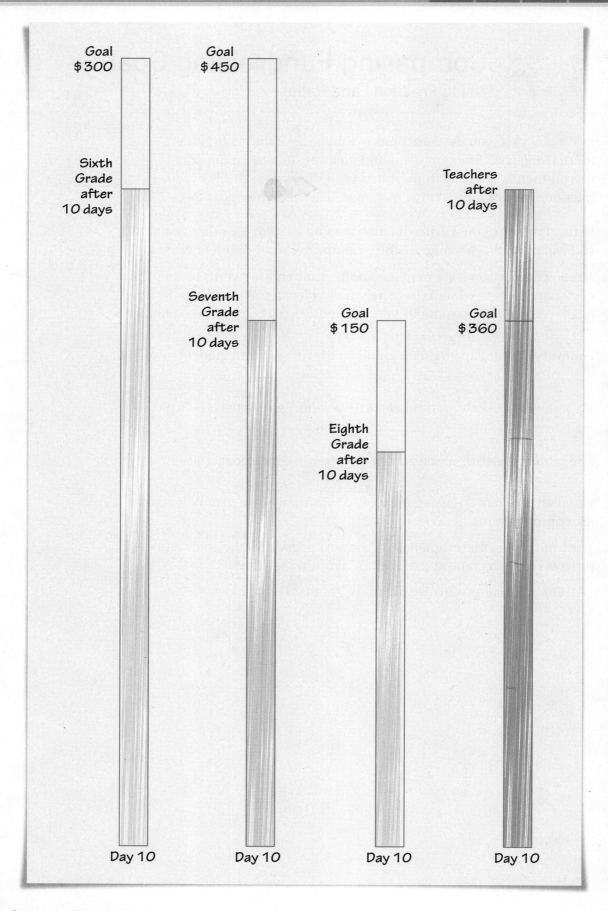

Goal
$300

Sixth
Grade
after
10 days

Goal
$450

Seventh
Grade
after
10 days

Teachers
after
10 days

Goal
$150

Goal
$360

Eighth
Grade
after
10 days

Day 10

Day 10

Day 10

Day 10

Problem 1.5

A 1. What fraction of its goal did each grade reach by the end of Day 10 of the fundraiser?

2. What fraction of their goal did the teachers reach by the end of Day 10 of the fundraiser?

3. How much money did each group raise?

B Margarita said: "I think the seventh graders raised $300 by the end of Day 10 because I wrote several fractions that are equivalent to what I found with my fraction strips: $\frac{2}{3}$."

$$\frac{2}{3} = \frac{4}{6} = \frac{20}{30} = \frac{60}{90} = \frac{300}{450}$$

Margarita also drew this picture.

150	150	150
$\frac{1}{3}$	$\frac{2}{3}$	$\frac{3}{3}$

1. Explain how Margarita found these equivalent fractions. How does her picture relate to her method of finding equivalent fractions?

2. Use equivalent fractions to show how much money the sixth graders had raised by the end of Day 10.

3. Use equivalent fractions to show how much money the teachers had raised by the end of Day 10.

continued on the next page >

Problem **1.5** continued

C 1. Brian wrote this comparison statement: The ratio of the amount of money raised by the sixth graders to the amount raised by the seventh graders is 250 : 300. Is this a correct statement? Explain.

2. Kate thought of $250 as 25 ten-dollar bills and $300 as 30 ten-dollar bills. She wrote the ratio, 25 : 30. Write a comparison statement using Kate's ratio.

3. Are Brian and Kate's two ratios equivalent? Explain.

4. What ratio would Kate write if she thought of $250 and $300 as numbers of fifty-dollar bills? Would thinking of twenty-dollar bills work? Explain.

5. Write two comparison statements, using equivalent ratios, for amounts of money raised by the sixth grade compared to the eighth grade in the fundraiser.

D On the last day of the fundraiser, the principal announces the results using both fractions and ratios. She has these two sticky notes on her desk.

$$\frac{250}{300} = \frac{5}{6}$$

$$250 : 300$$
or
$$5 : 6$$

1. What do you think is the meaning of each note?

2. When are fractions useful? When are ratios useful?

A C E Homework starts on page 27.

Applications

1. Another middle school conducted the same type of fundraiser as the middle school in the Problems. The banner below shows the goals for each grade.

   a. Write three statements that the principal could make when comparing the goals each grade has set.

   b. The teachers set a goal of $225. Write two statements the principal could use to compare this goal to the eighth graders' goal.

2. Bryce and Rachel are collecting canned goods for the local food bank. Bryce's goal is to collect 32 items. Rachel's goal is to collect 24 items. If Rachel and Bryce each meet their goal, what fraction of Bryce's goal does Rachel collect?

3. A sixth-grade class has 12 boys and 24 girls.

   a. Consider this statement: *For every 2 boys, there are 4 girls.* Do you agree with the statement? Explain.

   b. Write two more statements comparing the number of boys in the class to the number of girls.

4. In a different sixth-grade class, the ratio of boys to girls is 3 : 2. How many boys and how many girls could there be in this class? Is there more than one possible answer? Explain.

5. What fraction strips could you make if you started with a fourths strip?

6. Below is a number line labeled using an eighths strip. What other strips could label some of the marks on this number line?

For Exercises 7–9, copy each number line. Make and use fraction strips or use some other method to estimate and name the point with a fraction.

7.

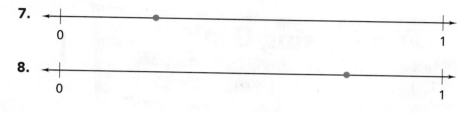

8.

9.

10. These students began to make a number line using different fraction strips as shown in the picture below. One student used the top fraction strip to mark $\frac{9}{12}$ on the number line.

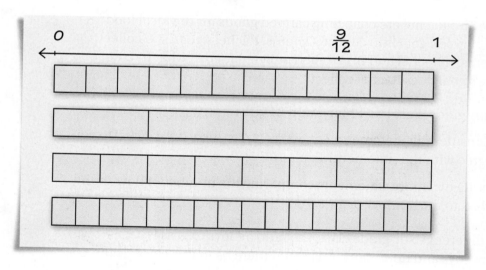

   a. Name three other fractions shown here that are equivalent to $\frac{9}{12}$.

   b. Name another fraction equivalent to $\frac{9}{12}$.

11. Erin used a fifths strip to mark and label $\frac{1}{5}$, $\frac{2}{5}$, $\frac{3}{5}$, and $\frac{4}{5}$ on her number line, as shown below.

    a. Why is no label needed for $\frac{5}{5}$?

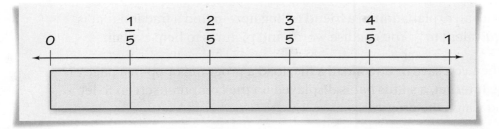

    b. Sally marked her fraction strip like this.

$\frac{1}{5}$	$\frac{1}{5}$	$\frac{1}{5}$	$\frac{1}{5}$	$\frac{1}{5}$

She says any two segments on her strip are the same as $\frac{2}{5}$. Do you agree with her? Explain how Sally's thinking is different from the way the number line is marked with $\frac{2}{5}$.

    c. If you label marks for $\frac{1}{10}$, $\frac{2}{10}$, $\frac{3}{10}$, $\frac{4}{10}$, $\frac{5}{10}$, $\frac{6}{10}$, $\frac{7}{10}$, $\frac{8}{10}$, $\frac{9}{10}$, and $\frac{10}{10}$ on Erin's number line, which marks now have more than one label? Why is this?

    d. If you were to extend your number line to reach from 0 to 2, there would be five fifths for every whole number length. What are some other "for every" statements you can make about a number line from 0 to 2?

For Exercises 12–15, decide whether the statement is correct or incorrect. Explain your reasoning in words or by drawing pictures.

12. $\frac{1}{3} = \frac{4}{12}$　　　　　　　　**13.** $\frac{4}{6} = \frac{2}{3}$

14. $\frac{2}{5} = \frac{1}{3}$　　　　　　　　**15.** $\frac{2}{5} = \frac{5}{10}$

For Exercises 16 and 17, use fraction strips to make marks on a number line to show that the two fractions are equivalent.

16. $\frac{2}{5}$ and $\frac{6}{15}$ **17.** $\frac{1}{9}$ and $\frac{2}{18}$

18. Write an explanation to a friend telling how to find a fraction that is equivalent to $\frac{3}{5}$. You can use words and pictures to help explain.

19. When you save or download a file, load a program, or open a page on the Internet, a status bar is displayed on the computer screen to let you watch the progress.

    a. Use the fraction strips shown to find three fractions that describe the status of the work in progress.

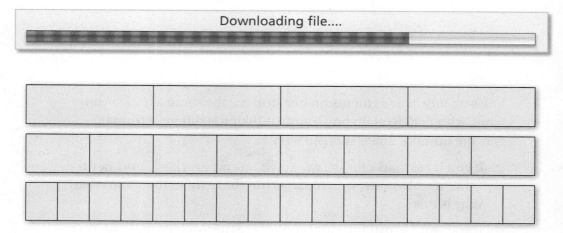

    b. Suppose that you are downloading a movie with a file size of 2.8 GB (gigabyte). If the status bar above indicates how much of the movie has been downloaded, how many gigabytes have been downloaded so far?

20. Use your fraction strips to locate and label these numbers on a number line: 0, $\frac{3}{4}$, and $\frac{7}{8}$. Then use your fraction strips to measure the distance between $\frac{3}{4}$ and $\frac{7}{8}$.

For Exercises 21 and 22, fold new fraction strips or use some other method to estimate the fraction of the fundraising thermometer that is shaded.

21.

Goal
$400

22.

Goal
$400

For Exercises 23–27, use this illustration of a drink dispenser. The gauge on the front of the dispenser shows how much of the liquid remains in the dispenser. The dispenser holds 120 cups.

23. **a.** About what fraction of the dispenser is filled with liquid?

   b. About how many cups of liquid are in the dispenser?

   c. About what fraction of the dispenser is empty?

   d. About how many more cups of liquid would it take to fill the dispenser?

24. Multiple Choice Which gauge shows about 37 out of 120 cups remaining?

25. Multiple Choice Which gauge shows about 10 out of 120 cups remaining?

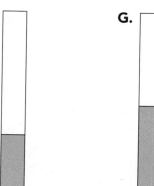

26. In Exercises 24 and 25, about what fraction is shaded in each gauge you chose?

27. For parts (a)–(c), sketch the gauge and, for each dispenser, say whether it can be best described as *almost empty, about half full,* or *almost full.*

   a. five sixths $\left(\frac{5}{6}\right)$ of a full dispenser

   b. three twelfths $\left(\frac{3}{12}\right)$ of a full dispenser

   c. five eighths $\left(\frac{5}{8}\right)$ of a full dispenser

28. If a class collects $155 toward a fundraising goal of $775, what fraction represents their progress toward their goal?

For Exercises 29–32, use the graphic below. Christopher downloads two different podcasts each day. Today, one file is loading more slowly than the other.

The Mathcast

45 MB of 60 MB - 22 seconds remaining

Fraction Podcast

20 MB of 30 MB - 1 minute remaining

29. What fraction of each file has downloaded so far?

30. Write a comparison statement for the sizes of the two files.

31. Write a comparison statement for the sizes of the downloaded parts of the two files.

32. How long will it take for each file to download, from beginning to end?

33. Dan, Karim, and Shawn are training for the school cross-country team. One day, they report the distances they ran as comparison statements.

   a. Dan says he ran twice as far as Karim. Give three possibilities for the distances each could have run.

   b. Karim says that the ratio of the distance he ran to the distance Shawn ran is 4 : 3. Give three possibilities for the distances each could have run.

   c. Which boy ran the furthest?

34. Kate, Sue, and Lisa are on the school basketball team. After one game, they report their scoring as comparison statements.

   a. Kate and Sue made the same number of successful shots as each other. Kate's successful shots were all 3-pointers. Sue's successful shots were all 2-pointers. Give three possibilities for the numbers of points each could have scored.

   b. Lisa says that she made twice as many successful shots as Sue but scored the same number of points. How is this possible?

   c. Which girl scored the most points?

   d. Which girl made the most shots?

Connections

For Exercises 35–38, explain your answer to each question.

35. Is 450 divisible by 5, 9, and 10?

36. Is 12 a divisor of 48?

37. Is 4 a divisor of 150?

38. Is 3 a divisor of 51?

39. Multiple Choice Choose the number that is *not* a factor of 300.

   A. 5

   B. 6

   C. 8

   D. 20

40. Multiple Choice Choose the answer that shows all of the factors of 48.

   F. 2, 4, 8, 24, and 48

   G. 1, 2, 3, 4, 5, 6, 8, and 12

   H. 48, 96, and 144

   J. 1, 2, 3, 4, 6, 8, 12, 16, 24, and 48

For Exercises 41–43, use the bar graph below, which shows the number of cans of juice three sixth-grade classes drank.

Sixth-Grade Juice Consumption

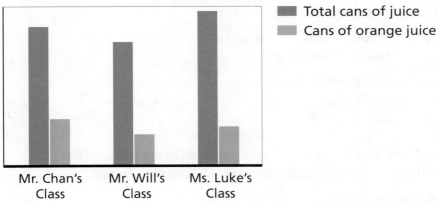

Total cans of juice
Cans of orange juice

Mr. Chan's
Class

Mr. Will's
Class

Ms. Luke's
Class

41. In each class, what fraction of the cans were orange juice?

42. In which class would you say orange juice was most popular?

43. **a.** Students in Mr. Chan's class drank a total of ten cans of orange juice. About how many cans of orange juice did the students in each of the other two classes drink?

   b. About how many total cans of juice did each of the three classes drink?

44. **a.** Miguel says that you can easily separate numbers divisible by 2 into two equal parts. Do you agree? Why or why not?

   b. Manny says that if Miguel is correct, then you can easily separate numbers divisible by 3 into three equal parts. Do you agree? Why or why not?

   c. Lupe says that if any number is divisible by n, you can easily separate it into n equal parts. Do you agree with her? Explain.

45. **a.** If you had a fraction strip folded into twelfths, what fractional lengths could you measure with the strip?

   b. How is your answer in part (a) related to the factors of 12?

46. **a.** If you had a fraction strip folded into tenths, what fractional lengths could you measure with the strip?

   b. How is your answer in part (a) related to the factors of 10?

47. Ricky found a beetle that is one fourth $\left(\frac{1}{4}\right)$ the length of the fraction strips used in Problem 1.3.

    a. How many beetle bodies, placed end to end, would have a total length equal to the length of a fraction strip?

    b. How many beetle bodies, placed end to end, would have a total length equal to three fraction strips?

    c. Ricky drew 13 paper beetle bodies, end to end, each the same length as the one he found. How many fraction strips long is Ricky's line of beetle bodies?

48. Rachel looked at the two ratios 25 : 30 and 250 : 300. In each ratio she noticed that the first and second numbers have a common factor.

    a. What are some common factors of 25 and 30?

    b. What are some common factors of 250 and 300?

    c. Rachel says that the two numbers in a ratio will always have a common factor. Is she correct?

49. Abby looked at the same ratios (25 : 30 and 250 : 300). In these two equivalent ratios, she noticed that the first numbers have a common factor and the second numbers have a different common factor.

    a. What are some common factors of 25 and 250?

    b. What are some common factors of 30 and 300?

    c. Abby says that the first numbers in two equivalent ratios will always have a common factor. Is she correct?

For Exercises 50 and 51, write a fraction to describe how much pencil is left, compared to a new pencil. Measure from the left edge of the eraser to the point of the pencil.

50.

51.

52. These bars represent trips that Ms. Axler took in her job this week.

300 km [ ]

180 km [ ]

200 km [ ]

a. Copy each bar and shade in the distance Ms. Axler traveled after going one third of the total distance for each trip.

b. How many kilometers had Ms. Axler traveled when she was at the one-third point in each trip? Explain your reasoning.

53. Brett and Jim sign up to run in the Memorial Day race in their town. There are two different events at this race, a 5K (5 kilometers) and a 10K (10 kilometers). Brett signed up for the 5K and Jim signed up for the 10K.

a. Make fraction strips where each kilometer run is partitioned on equal length fraction strips for both Brett and Jim.

b. Use thermometers to indicate when both Brett and Jim have finished $\frac{3}{5}$ of their races. How many kilometers has each person run at this point?

c. Use the thermometers to indicate when both Brett and Jim are finished with four kilometers of their races. What fraction represents the amount of their respective races they have finished?

d. Write a "for every" claim that relates the distances Brett and Jim have run to their distance goals.

54. A sprinter finished a 100-meter race in a time of 12.63 seconds.

    a. If the sprinter were able to keep the same rate of speed, how long would it take him to complete the 10,000-meter race?

    b. A long-distance runner won first place in the 10,000-meter race with a time of 37 minutes, 30 seconds. What is the time difference between the long-distance runner's actual time and the sprinter's hypothetical time from part (a)?

55. Multiple Choice Find the least common multiple of the following numbers: 3, 4, 5, 6, 10, and 15.

    A. 1   **B.** 15

    C. 60   **D.** 54,000

56. Use what you found in Exercise 55. Write the following fractions in equivalent form, all with the same denominator.

$$\frac{1}{3} \quad \frac{1}{4} \quad \frac{1}{5} \quad \frac{1}{6} \quad \frac{1}{10} \quad \frac{1}{15}$$

For Exercises 57–60, find the greatest common factor of each pair of numbers.

57. 12 and 48   **58.** 6 and 9

59. 24 and 72   **60.** 18 and 45

For Exercises 61–64, use your answers from Exercises 57–60 to write a fraction equivalent to each fraction given.

61. $\frac{12}{48}$ **62.** $\frac{6}{9}$ **63.** $\frac{24}{72}$ **64.** $\frac{18}{45}$

Extensions

For Exercises 65–67, write a numerator for each fraction to make the fraction close to, but not equal to, $\frac{1}{2}$. Then, write another numerator to make each fraction close to, but greater than, 1.

65. $\dfrac{\blacksquare}{22}$ **66.** $\dfrac{\blacksquare}{43}$ **67.** $\dfrac{\blacksquare}{17}$

For Exercises 68–70, write a denominator to make each fraction close to, but not equal to, $\frac{1}{2}$. Then, write another denominator to make each fraction close to, but greater than, 1.

68. $\dfrac{22}{\blacksquare}$ **69.** $\dfrac{43}{\blacksquare}$ **70.** $\dfrac{17}{\blacksquare}$

For Exercises 71–74, copy the number line. Use your knowledge of fractions to estimate and name the point with a fraction.

71.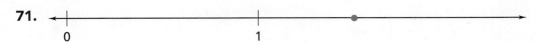

72.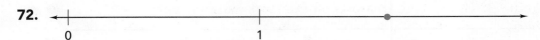

73.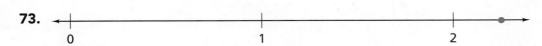

74.

For Exercises 75–80, copy the number line. Estimate and mark where the number 1 belongs on each number line.

75.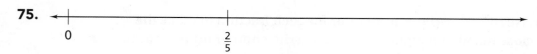

76.

77.

78.

79.

80.

81. Dario made three pizzas, which he sliced into quarters. After considering how many people he would be sharing with, he thought to himself, "Each person can have half."

   a. Is it possible that there was only one other person to share with? Explain.

   b. Is it possible that Dario was sharing the pizzas with 5 other people? Explain.

   c. Is it possible that Dario was sharing the pizzas with 11 other people? Explain.

82. In Problem 1.5, the eighth-grade thermometer is smaller than the sixth- and seventh-grade thermometers. Redraw the eighth-grade thermometer so that it is the same size as the sixth- and seventh-grade thermometers, but still shows the correct fraction for Day 10.

In your work in this Investigation, you wrote comparison statements using fractions and ratios. You also used fraction strips to make a number line and compare fractions. These questions will help you summarize what you have learned.

Think about your answers to these questions. Discuss your ideas with other students and your teacher. Then write a summary of your findings in your notebook.

1. **a. Write** three comparison statements about the same situation, one using difference, one using a fraction, and one using a ratio.

   b. Explain what you think a ratio is.

2. **a. What** does it mean for two fractions to be equivalent? For two ratios to be equivalent?

   b. What are some useful ways of finding equivalent fractions and equivalent ratios?

Common Core Mathematical Practices

As you worked on the Problems in this Investigation, you used prior knowledge to make sense of them. You also applied Mathematical Practices to solve the Problems. Think back over your work, the ways you thought about the Problems, and how you used Mathematical Practices.

Sophie described her thoughts in the following way:

We used fraction strips and number lines as a tool in Problem 1.3 to compare fractions and to find groups of fractions related to each other.

When we lined up the fraction strips, we noticed that equivalent fractions occurred when the fold marks lined up with each other and that these were all names for the same point on the line.

Common Core Standards for Mathematical Practice
MP5 Use appropriate tools strategically

• What other Mathematical Practices can you identify in Sophie's reasoning?

• Describe a Mathematical Practice that you and your classmates used to solve a different Problem in this Investigation.

2

Connecting Ratios and Rates

In Investigation 1, you used fraction strips as a tool to determine the fraction of each fundraising goal reached and locate points and distances on a number line. You also used ratios to compare quantities and checked to see if they were equivalent. In this Investigation you will continue to explore ratios and ways to write equivalent ratios.

The ratio statements in Investigation 1 were written as "for every" or "to" statements. Ratios can be written in many different ways.

Suppose the cost for ten students to go on a field trip is $120. You can write ratios to show how the quantities are related.

10 students *for every* $120

10 students *to every* $120

10 students : $120

Common Core State Standards

6.RP.A.3 Use ratio and rate reasoning to solve real-world and mathematical problems, e.g., by reasoning about tables of equivalent ratios, tape diagrams, double number line diagrams, or equations.

6.RP.A.3a Make tables of equivalent ratios relating quantities with whole-number measurements, find missing values in the tables . . .

6.RP.A.3b Solve unit rate problems including those involving unit pricing and constant speed.

Also 6.RP.A.1, 6.RP.A.2, 6.NS.B.4

Ratio statements can also be written as "per" statements. For example, "It costs $120 per 10 students to go on the trip." An equivalent comparison statement is "the cost per student to go on a field trip is $12." Now you can say

$12 *for every* 1 student

$12 *for each* student

$12 *per* student

This particular comparison, cost per one student, is called a unit rate. A **unit rate** is a comparison in which one of the numbers being compared is 1 unit.

• If the cost of food is $250 for 50 students, what is the cost per student?

To answer this question, you find the unit rate.

2.1 Equal Shares
Introducing Unit Rates

Often we share food so that each person gets the same amount. This may mean that food is cut into smaller pieces. Think about how to share a chewy fruit worm that is already marked in equal-sized pieces.

The chewy fruit worm below shows four equal segments.

How can you share this 4-segment chewy fruit worm equally among four people?

How many segments of the worm does each person get?

OR

How can you share this 4-segment chewy fruit worm equally among three people?

How many segments of the worm does each person get?

Problem 2.1

In Questions A and B, find the fraction of a chewy fruit worm each person gets.

A **1.** Show two ways that four people can share a 6-segment chewy fruit worm. In each case, how many segments does each person get?

2. Show two ways that six people can share an 8-segment chewy fruit worm. In each case, how many segments does each person get?

B **1.** Show how 12 people can share an 8-segment chewy fruit worm. How many segments are there for every person?

2. Show how five people can share a 3-segment chewy fruit worm. How much is this per person?

C Jena wants to share a 6-segment chewy fruit worm. The tape diagram below shows the marks she made on the worm so she can share it equally among the members in her CMP group.

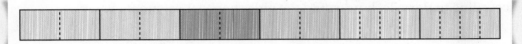

1. How many people are in her group?

2. Is there more than one possible answer to part (1)? Explain.

3. What is the number of segments per person?

4. Write a fraction to show the part of the chewy fruit worm each person gets.

D Would you rather be one of four people sharing a 6-segment chewy fruit worm or one of eight people sharing a 12-segment chewy fruit worm? Explain.

E Look back at your work on this Problem. Describe how you found or used unit rates.

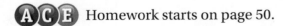 Homework starts on page 50.

2.2 Unequal Shares
Using Ratios and Fractions

Sometimes there are reasons to share quantities *unequally*. Suppose your older brother paid more than half the cost of a video game. You might think it is fair for him to spend more time playing the game. At a party, you might agree that your friend should take the bigger piece of chocolate cake because your friend likes chocolate more than you do.

Two sisters, Crystal and Alexa, are going to a strange birthday party. Instead of birthday cake, pairs of party guests are each served a large chewy fruit worm to share according to their ages. Since the sisters are not the same age, they do not share their fruit worm equally.

Crystal is 12 years old and Alexa is 6 years old. Their chewy fruit worm has 18 segments. According to their ages, Crystal gets 12 segments and Alexa gets 6 segments. The ratio of the girls' shares of the worm, 12 to 6, is equivalent to the ratio of their ages, 12 to 6.

- According to the rule, how would the girls share a 9-segment chewy fruit worm?

Since Crystal's age is two times Alexa's age, Crystal gets twice as many segments as Alexa. The ratio of Crystal's segments to Alexa's segments is 12 to 6 or 2 to 1.

- The ratio 2 to 1 is a unit rate. What do the numbers 2 and 1 mean for the sisters?

In this Problem you will explore situations that involve fractions and ratios.

Problem 2.2

Ⓐ Draw some chewy fruit worms with different numbers of segments that Crystal and Alexa can share without having to make new cuts.

Ⓑ **1.** Jared is 10 years old. His brother Peter is 15 years old. What are some chewy fruit worms they can share without having to make new cuts?

2. For each worm you described in part (1), write a ratio comparing the number of segments Jared gets to the number of segments Peter gets.

3. Are the ratios you wrote in part (2) equivalent to each other? Explain.

4. How would you write a unit rate to compare how many segments Jared and Peter get?

Ⓒ **1.** Caleb and Isaiah are brothers. They share a 14-segment chewy fruit worm according to their age. How old could they be?

2. Caleb gets 8 out of the 14 segments of the chewy fruit worm, so he gets $\frac{8}{14}$ and Isaiah gets $\frac{6}{14}$ of the worm.

a. From Question A, what fractions of the chewy fruit worm do Crystal and Alexa each get at the birthday party?

b. From Question B, what fractions of the chewy fruit worm do Jared and Peter each get at the birthday party?

c. How does the ratio of segments that Caleb and Isaiah get relate to the fractions of the chewy fruit worm that they each get?

ⒶⒸⒺ Homework starts on page 50.

2.3   Making Comparisons With Rate Tables

When comparing how to share chewy fruit worms, Crystal recorded how many segments she and her sister would get for different sizes of chewy fruit worms. Crystal thought she could use what she knew about equivalence to make a table showing the amounts.

Comparing Segments

Segments for Alexa	6	3	1	2	$\frac{1}{2}$	10
Segments for Crystal	12	6	2	4	1	20

The table shows that for every segment given to Alexa, Crystal gets two segments. This is Alexa's unit rate. The table also shows that for every $\frac{1}{2}$ segment Alexa is given, Crystal gets one segment. This is Crystal's unit rate.

Crystal sees an ad for chewy fruit worms. She decides she wants the student council to include chewy fruit worms in the fundraising sale.

You can use the information in the advertisement to compute the price for any number of worms you want to buy. One way to figure out the price of a single item from a quantity price is use the information to build a **rate table** of equivalent ratios.

The rate table in Question A shows the price for different numbers of chewy fruit worms. The cost of 30 chewy fruit worms is $3.

Problem 2.3

A 1. Crystal wants to calculate costs quickly for many different numbers of chewy fruit worms. Copy and complete the rate table below with prices for each of the numbers of chewy fruit worms.

Chewy Fruit Worm Pricing

Number of Worms	1	5	10	15	30	90	150	180
Reduced Price	▪	▪	▪	▪	$3	▪	▪	▪

2. How much do 3 chewy fruit worms cost? 300 chewy fruit worms?

3. How many chewy fruit worms can you buy for $50? For $10?

4. What is the unit price of one chewy fruit worm? What is the unit rate?

B The student council also decides to sell popcorn to raise money. One ounce of popcorn (unpopped) kernels yields 4 cups of popcorn. One serving is a bag of popcorn that holds 2 cups of popcorn.

1. Use a rate table to find the number of ounces of popcorn kernels needed to determine the cups of popcorn.

Cups of Popcorn From Ounces of Kernels

Number of Cups of Popcorn	4	▪	▪	▪	▪	▪	▪	▪	▪	▪	▪	▪
Number of Ounces of Popcorn Kernels	1	2	3	4	5	6	7	8	9	10	11	12

2. How many cups of popcorn can you make from 12 ounces of popcorn kernels? From 30 ounces of popcorn kernels?

3. How many ounces of popcorn kernels are needed to make 40 cups of popcorn? To make 100 cups of popcorn?

4. How many ounces of kernels are needed to make 100 servings?

5. How many ounces of kernels are needed to make 1 cup?

C 1. How do rate tables help you answer Question A and Question B?

2. How do unit rates help you answer Question A and Question B?

 Homework starts on page 50.

Applications

1. Show two ways three people can share a 5-segment chewy fruit worm.

2. Show two ways five people can share a 3-segment chewy fruit worm.

3. Sharon is ready to share the 4-segment chewy fruit worm shown below. She has already made the marks she needs so that she can share it equally among the members of her group.

   a. Give two different numbers of people that could be in Sharon's group.

   b. For each answer you gave in part (a), write a ratio comparing the number of people sharing a chewy fruit worm to the number of segments they are sharing. How would you rewrite this as a unit rate?

4. Cheryl, Rita, and four of their friends go to a movie and share a 48-ounce bag of popcorn equally and three 48-inch licorice laces equally. Write a ratio comparing the number of ounces of popcorn to the number of friends. Then, write a unit rate comparing the length of licorice lace for each person.

5. The Lappans buy three large sandwiches to serve at a picnic. Nine people come to the picnic. Show three different ways to cut the sandwiches so that each person gets an equal share.

6. Three neighbors are sharing a rectangular strip of land for a garden. They divide the land into 24 equal-sized pieces. They each get the same amount of land. Write a ratio comparing the number of pieces of land to the number of people. Write the answer in more than one way.

7. For each chewy fruit worm below write the possible ages of the two people sharing the worm by age.

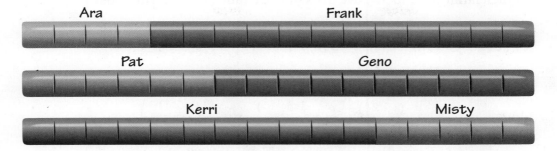

Use this information for Exercises 8–10. At the birthday party in Problem 2.2, the children run relay races. The distance each team member runs depends on the ratio of their ages. For example, a boy who is twice as old as a girl runs twice as far.

8. Crystal is 12 years old and Alexa is 6 years old. If Crystal runs 100 yards, how far does Alexa run? How far do they run altogether?

9. Jared is 10 years old and Peter is 15 years old. Together, they run 150 yards. How far does each brother run?

10. Wynne and Emmett are brother and sister. Wynne runs 180 yards. Emmett runs 120 yards. How old could each of them be?

Use this information for Exercises 11–14. Parents are older than their children. The ratio of a parent's age to a child's age changes as the parent and child get older.

11. Can a parent ever be exactly twice as old as his or her child? Explain.

12. Can a parent ever be exactly three times as old as his or her child? Explain.

13. Can the ratio of a parent's age to his or her child's age ever be exactly 3 : 2? Explain.

14. Can the ratio of a parent's age to his or her child's age ever be exactly 10 : 9? Explain.

15. Crystal and Alexa convince the older members of their family to break up the chewy fruit worms using age ratios. They want to know which family members have the same age ratio as Crystal and Alexa.

   a. Use the ages of their family members to find pairs that have the same age ratio as Crystal (age 12) and Alexa (age 6).

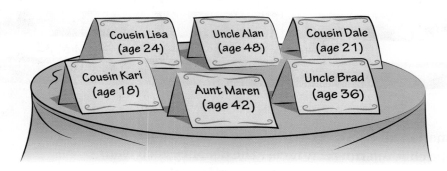

   Cousin Lisa (age 24)   Uncle Alan (age 48)   Cousin Dale (age 21)
   Cousin Kari (age 18)   Aunt Maren (age 42)   Uncle Brad (age 36)

   b. What do all the ratios that you wrote in part (a) have in common?

For Exercises 16–18, copy and complete the table comparing the chewy fruit worm segments each family member received. State both unit rates in each comparison.

16.

Segments for Alan	48	12	■	1	■	7
Segments for Lisa	24	■	8	■	1	■

17.

Segments for Lisa	24	12	■	1	■	■
Segments for Alexa	6	■	2	■	1	$1\frac{1}{2}$

18.

Segments for Alan	48	24	■	1	■	■
Segments for Alexa	6	■	2	■	1	$1\frac{1}{2}$

For Exercises 19–22, use the family members from Exercise 15, including Crystal and Alexa. Determine which two people have each age ratio.

19. The unit rate is 2 : 1.

20. The unit rate is 4 : 1.

21. The ratio of segments (ages) is 3 : 4.

22. The ratio of segments (ages) is 3 : 2.

For Exercises 23 and 24, Rosco is planning meals for his family. He uses the vertical rate tables.

23. **a.** Complete the rate table for the macaroni and cheese ingredients.

Macaroni and Cheese

Ounces of Macaroni	Cups of Cheese
8	1
▓	2
▓	3
▓	4
▓	5
▓	6

b. How many ounces of macaroni would you need for 7 cups of cheese?

c. How many cups of cheese would you need for 88 ounces of macaroni?

24. **a.** Complete the rate table for the spaghetti ingredients.

Spaghetti and Sauce

Ounces of Spaghetti	Ounces of Tomatoes
12	16
6	8
3	
2	▦
1	▦

b. What is the unit rate comparing the number of ounces of tomatoes to 1 ounce of spaghetti?

c. What is the unit rate comparing 1 ounce of tomatoes to the number of ounces of spaghetti?

Connections

25. Ursula, Ubaldo, Ulysses, and Dora were trying to come up with different ways to divide a 10-segment chewy fruit worm among the four of them. Which of these strategies would result in sharing equally?

- Ursula's Strategy:

  Give everyone two segments, and then divide the remaining two segments into four equal pieces with each person getting another half of a segment.

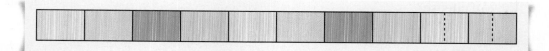

- Ubaldo's Strategy:

  Give each person one segment, then if there's at least four segments left, give each person another segment. Repeat this process until there are less than four segments, then cut the leftover pieces into four equal parts and give each person a part.

- Ulysses' Strategy:

  Give each person two segments, and then use a spinner to pick the winner of the extra two segments.

- Dora's Strategy:

  Forget about the segments. Just cut the worm in half, and then cut each half in half again.

26. If you were going to make segment marks on a chewy fruit worm without any marks, what would be the advantage or disadvantage of using a prime number of segments?

27. A typical container of orange juice concentrate holds 12 fluid ounces (fl oz). The standard recipe is "Mix one can of concentrate with three cans of cold water."

   a. What is the ratio of concentrate to water?

   b. How large of a container will you need to hold the juice?

   c. Olivia has a one-gallon container to fill with orange juice. She uses the standard recipe. How much concentrate does she need? (One gallon is 128 fl oz.)

28. A typical container of lemonade concentrate holds 12 fl oz. The standard recipe is "Mix one can of concentrate with $4\frac{1}{3}$ cans of cold water."

   a. What is the ratio of concentrate to water?

   b. How large of a container will you need to hold the lemonade?

   c. Olivia has a one-gallon container to fill with lemonade. She uses the standard recipe. How much concentrate does she need? (One gallon is 128 fl oz.)

29. Langhus Convenience Store sells multiple sizes of chewy fruit worms. Betsy, Emily, and John are trying to decide which of the deals would give them the most chewy fruit worms for the price.

Chewy Fruit Worms
LARGE SIZE
Price Reduced! 10 worms for $4
small size   medium size
28 worms for $12   18 worms for $8

a. Which argument do you think is the best? Explain.

- Betsy: The small size is the best deal because you get the most amount of worms, 10 more than the medium size, and 18 more than the large size.

- John: The large size is the best deal because you have to pay the least amount of money overall.

- Emily: I used the least common multiple of 4, 8, and 12, which is 24. For $24, I could buy 60 large worms, 54 medium worms, and 56 small worms. The large size is the best deal.

b. How could Betsy, John, and Emily use unit rates to find the best deal?

30. As Johann is working on unit rates in Exercises 16–24, he notices something interesting and says to his teacher, "Whenever you compare two quantities and you write both unit rates, at least one of them will have a fraction in it." Is Johann correct? Explain why you agree or disagree with him.

Extensions

For Exercises 31–33, consider the conjectures Jena made while working on Problem 2.1. Which conjectures do you think are true? Explain.

31. If the number of people is greater than the number of segments, each person will get less than one segment.

32. There are at least two ways to divide any chewy fruit worm so that everyone will get the same amount.

33. If the ratio of people to segments is 1 : 2, then each person will get $\frac{1}{2}$ of a segment.

34. Harold is eight years older than Maynard. On Harold's sixteenth birthday, he notices something interesting about their age ratios. He says, "When I was nine, the ratio of my age to Harold's was 9 : 1. A year later the ratio was 5 : 1. That's when I was ten and Maynard was two. Now on my sixteenth birthday, I'm twice as old as Maynard, which means the ratio of our ages is 2 : 1." Will Harold and Maynard ever have an age ratio 1 : 1? Explain.

35. A women's 4-by-100 meter medley relay team finished in second place. In the relay, each member swims 100 meters using a different stroke. The ages of the team members are 21, 22, 25, and 41.

The age difference between the oldest and youngest swimmer on this team was 20 years!

Suppose they had broken up the distance of 400 meters by age as in Problem 2.2. How far would each person swim in the relay?

36. Mariette, Melissa, and Michelle were given this follow-up question by Mr. Mirasola to Problem 2.3, "If you had $3.55, how many large chewy fruit worms could you buy?"

- Mariette said that she could buy $35\frac{1}{2}$.

- Melissa said that she could buy only 35.

- Michelle said that she could buy only 30.

  Mr. Mirasola said, "You are all correct depending on how you think of the ad." How is it possible that they could all be correct?

37. On a recent trip to Canada, Tomas learned that there was an "exchange rate" between U.S. dollars and Canadian dollars. When he exchanged his U.S. dollars, he did not get the same number of Canadian dollars back. Tomas hopes to visit many different countries one day, so he does some research and finds a Web site with some basic money conversions on it.

a. Find the unit rate for each country below.

Currency Exchange Rates

$20 US ≈ 19 Australian Dollars	$1 US ≈ ▮ AUD	$▮ US ≈ 1 AUD
$5 US ≈ 4 Euros	$1 US ≈ ▮ Euros	$▮ US ≈ 1 Euro
$50 US ≈ 49 Swiss Francs	$1 US ≈ ▮ SF	$▮ US ≈ 1 SF
$3 US ≈ 2 Pounds (UK)	$1 US ≈ ▮ Pounds	$▮ US ≈ 1 Pound
$4 US ≈ 5 Singapore Dollars	$1 US ≈ ▮ SGD	$▮ US ≈ 1 SGD

Note: Exchange rates often change from day to day; there are Web sites that have the most up-to-date exchange rates.

b. How can you use this information to convert euros to Australian dollars or Swiss francs to Singapore dollars? Explain.

5000 Japanese yen, Ichiyo Higuchi (1872–1896), writer and poet

10 US dollars, Andrew Jackson (1767–1845), seventh President

10 English pounds, Queen Elizabeth II (b. 1926)

20 Australian dollars, Mary Reibey (1777–1855), businesswoman

Mathematical Reflections

In this Investigation, you used ratios to share equally and unequally according to certain rules. You used rate tables and unit rates to solve problems. These questions will help you summarize what you have learned.

Think about your answers to these questions. Discuss your ideas with other students and your teacher. Then write a summary in your notebook.

1. **a. How** can you determine a unit rate for a situation?

   b. Describe some ways that unit rates are useful.

2. **a. What** strategies do you use to make a rate table?

   b. Describe some ways that rate tables are useful.

3. **How** are your strategies for writing equivalent ratios the same as or different from writing equivalent fractions?

Common Core Mathematical Practices

As you worked on the Problems in this Investigation, you used prior knowledge to make sense of the Problems. You also applied Mathematical Practices to solve the Problems. Think back over your work, the ways you thought about the Problems, and how you used Mathematical Practices.

Jayden described his thoughts in the following way:

We used rate tables to find the prices for different amounts of chewy fruit worms in Problem 2.3.

In the rate table, we noticed a repeated pattern such as "for every 5 worms we need to pay $ .50." Some of us expressed this pattern in the amount of a unit rate: the money per each worm or number of worms per $ 1.

In figuring out how much we need to pay for 300 worms, we used our rate table and noticed that there is a $ 3 increase for every 30 worms.

Common Core Standards for Mathematical Practice

MP7 Look for and make use of structure

 • What other Mathematical Practices can you identify in Jayden's reasoning?

• Describe a Mathematical Practice that you and your classmates used to solve a different Problem in this Investigation.

Investigation 3

Extending the Number Line

In this Unit, you have used fractions to express parts of a whole and ratios to compare quantities. In this Investigation, you will learn about negative fractions and improper fractions. You will also learn about the opposite and absolute value of a number. You will use this information to extend the number line to include negative numbers.

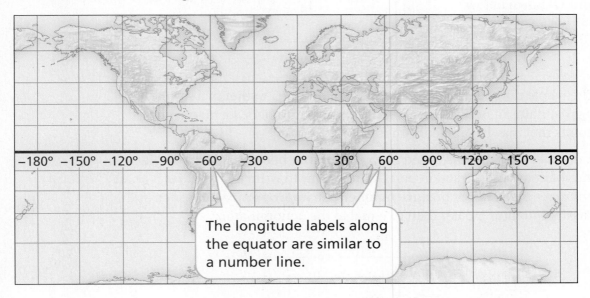

The longitude labels along the equator are similar to a number line.

Common Core State Standards

6.NS.C.6a Recognize opposite signs of numbers as indicating locations on opposite sides of 0 on the number line; recognize that the opposite of the opposite of a number is the number itself, e.g., $-(-3) = 3$, and that 0 is its own opposite.

6.NS.C.6c Find and position integers and other rational numbers on a horizontal or vertical number line diagram . . .

6.NS.C.7b Write, interpret, and explain statements of order for rational numbers in real-world contexts.

6.NS.C.7c Understand the absolute value of a rational number as its distance from 0 on the number line; interpret absolute value as magnitude for a positive or negative quantity in a real-world situation.

Also 6.RP.A.1, 6.RP.A.2, 6.RP.A.3, 6.NS.B.3, 6.NS.B.4, 6.NS.C.5, 6.NS.C.6, 6.NS.C.7, and 6.NS.C.7d

As you work through this Investigation, you will combine new information with your previous knowledge of the place-value system of whole numbers to study **decimals.**

In Investigation 2, you used a fraction strip model to show how an item could be shared among a group of people. In this Investigation, you will see how a fraction of an item can be expressed on a grid model. The grid model is also used to write fractions as decimals. In time, you will be able to identify when it is appropriate to express equal shares as a fraction or as a decimal.

3.1 Extending the Number Line
Integers and Mixed Numbers

In Investigation 1, you worked with the part of the number line between 0 and 1, shown below.

The whole numbers on a number line follow one another in a simple, regular pattern. Between every pair of whole numbers are many other points that may be labeled with fractions.

A number such as $1\frac{1}{2}$ is called a **mixed number** because it has a whole number part and a fraction part. Another way to write this number is as an *improper fraction*. For positive numbers, an **improper fraction** such as $\frac{3}{2}$ has a numerator greater than or equal to the denominator.

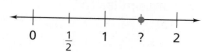

- Why can this point be labeled with two names: $1\frac{1}{2}$ and $\frac{3}{2}$?

There is really nothing improper about these fractions. This is just a name used for fractions that represent more than one whole. You may have used a mixed number or an improper fraction to express the teachers' fundraising success in the previous Investigation.

The number line can be extended in both directions, as shown below. Numbers to the left of zero are marked with a "−" sign and are read as *negative one, negative two,* etc.

In this Problem, you will use fractions, mixed numbers, and improper fractions. You can represent positive and negative fractions and mixed numbers as points on the number line.

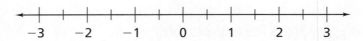

- Betty says that the mark between 2 and 3 should be labeled $\frac{1}{2}$. Do you agree?

- Judi says that the mark between 2 and 3 should be labeled $\frac{5}{2}$. Do you agree?

- What label should you put on the mark between −2 and −3?

- If there were a mark halfway between that mark and −2, what label would you put on it?

On the number line below, 5 and −5 are the same distance from 0 but in opposite directions. Therefore, 5 and −5 are **opposites.** The opposite of 5 is −5. The opposite of −5 is 5. Similarly, the opposite of $2\frac{1}{2}$ is $-2\frac{1}{2}$, and the opposite of $-2\frac{1}{2}$ is $2\frac{1}{2}$.

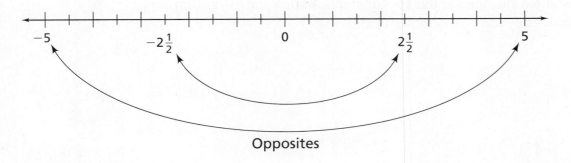

Opposites

The **absolute value** of a number is its distance from 0 on the number line. Numbers that are the same distance from 0 have the same absolute value. The absolute value of $2\frac{1}{2}$ and the absolute value of $-2\frac{1}{2}$ are both $2\frac{1}{2}$.

You can express the absolute value of a number two ways without words.

Absolute Value Bars

$$\left|2\frac{1}{2}\right| = 2\frac{1}{2}$$

$$\left|-2\frac{1}{2}\right| = 2\frac{1}{2}$$

OR

Calculator Notation

$$\text{abs}\left(2\frac{1}{2}\right) = 2\frac{1}{2}$$

$$\text{abs}\left(-2\frac{1}{2}\right) = 2\frac{1}{2}$$

- What is the opposite of $-\frac{2}{3}$? What is the opposite of $\frac{2}{3}$?
- What is the absolute value of $-\frac{2}{3}$? What is the absolute value of $\frac{2}{3}$?

Zero, whole numbers, fractions, and their opposites are **rational numbers.** The numbers $-\frac{9}{5}$, -3, 0, $\frac{2}{3}$, and $2\frac{1}{3}$ are all rational numbers.

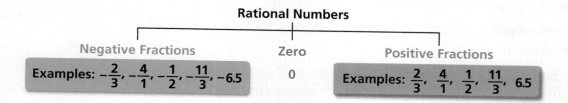

Rational Numbers

Negative Fractions

Examples: $-\frac{2}{3}$, $-\frac{4}{1}$, $-\frac{1}{2}$, $-\frac{11}{3}$, -6.5

Zero

0

Positive Fractions

Examples: $\frac{2}{3}$, $\frac{4}{1}$, $\frac{1}{2}$, $\frac{11}{3}$, 6.5

Negative numbers can also be improper fractions. Improper fractions have an absolute value greater than or equal to 1. Both $\frac{7}{5}$ and $-\frac{7}{5}$ are improper fractions. They can be written as $1\frac{2}{5}$ and $-1\frac{2}{5}$.

Problem 3.1

A 1. On a number line like the one below, mark and label these fractions.

$$\frac{1}{4} \quad \frac{2}{4} \quad \frac{3}{4} \quad \frac{4}{4} \quad \frac{5}{4} \quad \frac{6}{4} \quad \frac{7}{4} \quad \frac{8}{4} \quad \frac{9}{4} \quad \frac{0}{4} \quad -\frac{1}{4} \quad -\frac{2}{4} \quad -\frac{3}{4} \quad -\frac{4}{4} \quad -\frac{5}{4}$$

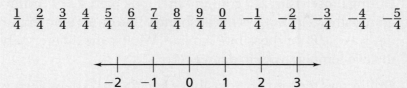

2. Which of the fractions can be written as mixed numbers? Explain.

B 1. On a new number line, mark and label these numbers.

$$\frac{1}{3} \quad 1\frac{1}{3} \quad 2\frac{2}{3} \quad 3 \quad 3\frac{1}{3} \quad -\frac{1}{3} \quad -1\frac{1}{3} \quad -1\frac{2}{3}$$

2. Which of these numbers can be written as improper fractions? Explain.

C 1. What is the opposite of $\frac{1}{2}$?

2. What is the opposite of the opposite of $\frac{1}{2}$?

3. What is the opposite of 0?

4. Write a mathematical sentence for each of the opposite statements in parts (1)–(3).

D 1. What numbers have an absolute value of 1?

2. How many numbers have an absolute value of $\frac{5}{4}$? What are the numbers?

3. How many numbers have an absolute value of 0?

continued on the next page >

Problem 3.1 continued

E **1.** **a.** Griffin visited her grandfather in Canada twice in the same year. During those visits, her grandmother took pictures of Griffin with her grandfather. Griffin says the absolute value of the temperature each day was 10. Is this possible? Explain. What is the difference between the two temperatures in degrees?

   b. Griffin says the bird's height above and the fish's depth below sea level are opposites. Is this possible? Explain.

2. Aaron is playing a game in which he earns points for a correct answer and loses the same number of points for an incorrect answer.

   a. Aaron has zero points. The next question is worth 300 points. Aaron says, "It doesn't matter whether I get the answer right or wrong, the absolute value of my score will be 300." Do you agree? Why or why not?

   b. Later in the game, Aaron's score is back to zero. He then answers two more questions and his score is back to zero again. What could be the point values of the last two questions?

 Homework starts on page 82.

3.2 Estimating and Ordering Rational Numbers

Comparing Fractions to Benchmarks

When you solve problems involving fractions and decimals, you may find it useful to estimate the size of the numbers. One way is to compare each positive fraction to 0, $\frac{1}{2}$, and 1. These numbers serve as **benchmarks,** or reference points. You also can compare each negative fraction to the opposites of the benchmarks: 0, $-\frac{1}{2}$, and -1. These benchmarks divide the number line below into six equal intervals: the interval between $-1\frac{1}{2}$ and -1, the interval between -1 and $-\frac{1}{2}$, and so on.

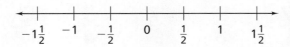

- Name a fraction close to, but not equal to $\frac{1}{2}$. Is it greater than or less than $\frac{1}{2}$?

- Name a fraction close to but not equal to $-\frac{1}{2}$. Is it greater than or less than $-\frac{1}{2}$?

- How can you decide which benchmark is closest to a given rational number?

Problem **3.2**

A **1.** Decide in which interval on the number line each fraction below is located.

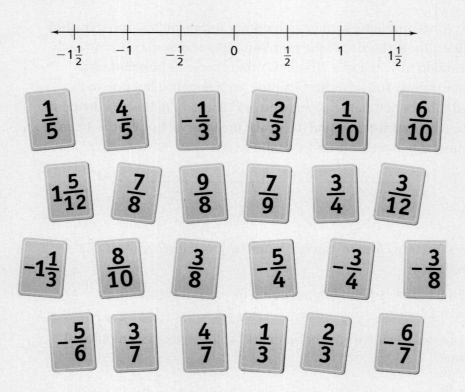

Record your information in a table like the one below that shows which fractions are in each interval.

$-1\frac{1}{2}$ to -1	-1 to $-\frac{1}{2}$	$-\frac{1}{2}$ to 0	0 to $\frac{1}{2}$	$\frac{1}{2}$ to 1	1 to $1\frac{1}{2}$
▪	▪	▪	▪	▪	▪

2. Decide whether each fraction above is closest to $-1\frac{1}{2}$, -1, $-\frac{1}{2}$, 0, $\frac{1}{2}$, 1, or $1\frac{1}{2}$.

Record your information in a way that also includes the possibility that some fractions are exactly halfway between two benchmarks.

Problem **3.2** *continued*

B Insert a less than ($<$), greater than ($>$), or equal to ($=$) symbol in each sentence below. Explain how the numbers or the number line helped you decide.

1. $-\frac{5}{2}$ ■ 3

2. 0 ■ -3

3. $-\frac{5}{3}$ ■ $-\frac{11}{2}$

4. Callum says that every number is greater than its opposite. Do you agree? Explain.

5. Blake says that he can use absolute value to help order the numbers $-\frac{6}{5}$ and $-\frac{2}{3}$. He says the absolute value of $-\frac{6}{5}$ is greater so it is farther away from zero, and therefore $-\frac{6}{5} < -\frac{2}{3}$. Do you agree? Explain.

6. Will Blake's strategy work for all of the comparisons you did in Questions 1–3? Explain.

C Compare each pair of fractions using benchmarks and other strategies. Then copy the fractions and insert a less than ($<$), greater than ($>$), or equal to ($=$) symbol. Describe your strategies.

1. $\frac{5}{8}$ ■ $\frac{6}{8}$

2. $\frac{5}{6}$ ■ $\frac{5}{8}$

3. $\frac{2}{3}$ ■ $\frac{3}{9}$

4. $\frac{13}{12}$ ■ $\frac{6}{5}$

5. $-\frac{3}{4}$ ■ $\frac{2}{5}$

6. $-1\frac{1}{5}$ ■ $-1\frac{1}{3}$

D The smartphone screen shows deposits to and withdrawals from Brian's checking account.

Online Checking Account		
10/09/2013	Giancarlo's Steakhouse	−50
10/14/2013	Deposit Broad St.	100
10/21/2013	Barbara's Bookstore	−32
10/23/2013	Deposit Maplewood Ave.	32
10/27/2013	Waterstone Hardware	−30

1. Which account activities have the same absolute value? What information does this provide for Brian?

2. Brian says that he spent less money on October 27th than he did on October 21st because the absolute value of the account withdrawal is closer to zero. Do you agree? Explain.

 Homework starts on page 82.

3.3 Sharing 100 Things
Using Tenths and Hundredths

You see decimals every day, in lots of different places.

- Where might you find each of the decimal numbers below?

Decimals give people a way to write fractions with denominators of 10 or 100 or 1,000 or 10,000 or even 100,000,000,000, as in the table below. These denominators are different forms of **base ten numeration.**

Fraction	Denominator as a Power of 10	Decimal
$\frac{1}{10}$	$\frac{1}{10^1}$	0.1
$\frac{1}{100}$	$\frac{1}{10^2}$	0.01
$\frac{1}{1,000}$	$\frac{1}{10^3}$	0.001
$\frac{1}{10,000}$	$\frac{1}{10^4}$	0.0001
$\frac{1}{100,000}$	$\frac{1}{10^5}$	0.00001
$\frac{1}{1,000,000}$	$\frac{1}{10^6}$	0.000001
$\vdots$	$\vdots$	$\vdots$
$\frac{1}{100,000,000,000}$	?	?

In Investigation 1, you folded fraction strips. One of the strips you made was a tenths strip, similar to the one shown below.

- How could you fold or mark the tenths strip to get a hundredths strip?

- How would you label each part of this new fraction strip?

A tenths grid is also divided into 10 equal parts. You can further divide a tenths grid by drawing horizontal lines to make 100 parts. This is called a hundredths grid.

Tenths Grid   **Hundredths Grid**

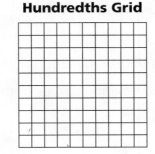

You can represent fractions on grids. You can write fractional parts of 100 as decimal numbers.

Fraction	Decimal	Representation on a Hundredths Grid
$\frac{5}{10}$	0.5	
$\frac{20}{100}$	0.20	
$\frac{2}{100}$	0.02	

? How can you make and shade a grid to show the following fractional and decimal amounts?

Fraction	Decimal
$\frac{20}{100}$	0.2
■	0.20
$\frac{250}{1,000}$	■

- What are some fractions and decimals equivalent to $\frac{3}{10}$?
- Do 0.20, 0.02, and 0.2 all represent the same number? Explain.

Problem 3.3

Wendy's mother Ann makes lasagna every year to celebrate the winter holiday season. She makes the lasagna in an enormous 20 inch-by-20 inch square pan.

Ann cuts the lasagna into 100 servings to share with friends, family, neighbors, and co-workers. You may use grids to help answer the following questions.

A Ann gave one pan of lasagna to her ten co-workers.

1. If the co-workers share the lasagna equally, how many servings will each co-worker get? Write each person's share as a fractional and a decimal part of a pan.

2. Ann's pan is 20 inches by 20 inches. Describe each co-worker's share of the lasagna.

B Ann baked three more pans of lasagna. Each pan was shared with a different group of people. For each group below,

- write each person's share as a number of servings.

- write each person's share as a fractional and decimal part of a pan.

1. One pan was shared among Wendy's four favorite teachers.

2. Ann miscalculated and had only one pan to share among all 200 sixth-graders at Wendy's school.

3. One pan went to eight of Ann's neighbors.

continued on the next page >

Problem **3.3** *continued*

C **1.** Four is a good number of people for Ann to share her lasagna with because she does not have to subdivide the 100 servings into even smaller pieces to share equally. What are some other numbers of people that Ann could share with without having to cut her servings into smaller pieces? Describe any patterns you find.

2. What are some numbers of people that force Ann to subdivide the 100 servings into smaller pieces? Explain.

D Sonam compared the decimal numbers 0.1 and 0.09 by thinking about lasagna. She said that 0.1 represents one serving of Ann's lasagna and 0.09 represents 9 servings, so 0.09 > 0.1. What do you think? Explain your reasoning.

 Homework starts on page 82.

3.4 Decimals on the Number Line

In Problem 3.3, you thought about a pan of lasagna that was cut into 100 pieces, and you considered relationships between the fractional and decimal representations for different numbers of servings.

The place value chart on the next page shows the names of each position relative to the decimal point. Think about these questions as you look at it:

- What do you notice about the fraction names of each place value as you move to the right from the decimal point?

- Why are these names useful in writing fractions as decimals?

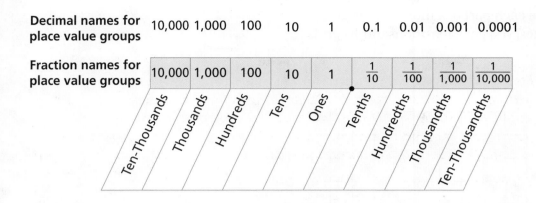

Decimal names for place value groups	10,000	1,000	100	10	1	0.1	0.01	0.001	0.0001
Fraction names for place value groups	10,000	1,000	100	10	1	$\frac{1}{10}$	$\frac{1}{100}$	$\frac{1}{1,000}$	$\frac{1}{10,000}$
	Ten-Thousands	Thousands	Hundreds	Tens	Ones	Tenths	Hundredths	Thousandths	Ten-Thousandths

It is often useful to divide a whole into more than 100 pieces. When working with decimals you can always divide the whole into smaller pieces, but you must always use a divisor that is a power of 10.

For example, you made a tenths strip in Investigation 1. You can fold or mark the tenths strip to get a hundredths strip.

Similarly, you saw the hundredths grids in Problem 3.3. If each square in a hundredths grid is divided into 10 pieces, you get a thousandths grid.

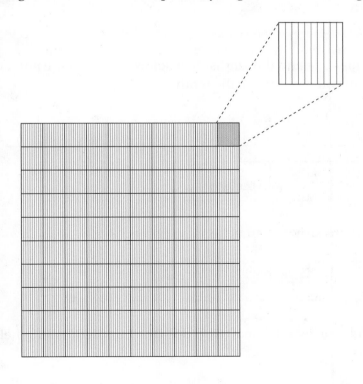

If you divide each part of a thousandths grid into 10 pieces, you get a ten-thousandths grid.

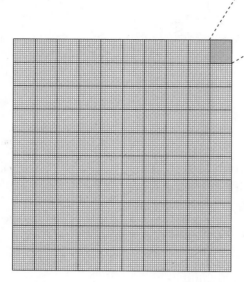

- How can you use decimal notation to write amounts such as $12\frac{1}{2}$ hundredths of a pan of lasagna?

Problem 3.4

A **1.** Use the number line and the tenths strip below. Which of the points $\frac{1}{4}$, $\frac{2}{4}$, $\frac{3}{4}$, and $\frac{4}{4}$ can you name using the tenths strip?

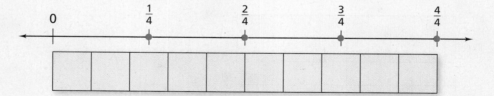

2. Use a hundredths strip to name the same points.

3. Write each fraction as a decimal. How does the hundredths strip help you to do this?

Problem **3.4** *continued*

B **1.** **a.** Which of the fractions below could be written with tenths or hundredths in the denominator? For each such fraction, write an equivalent decimal.

$$\frac{1}{3} \qquad \frac{1}{5} \qquad \frac{2}{5} \qquad \frac{2}{6} \qquad \frac{3}{6} \qquad \frac{1}{8} \qquad \frac{63}{50} \qquad \frac{112}{200}$$

   b. Which fractions cannot be written with tenths or hundredths in the denominator? Justify your answer.

2. Name two other fractions that are easy to write as equivalent decimals, and two that are not easy to write as decimals. Explain.

3. **a.** Which decimal is closest to $\frac{1}{3}$: 0.3, 0.33 or 0.333? Explain.

   b. Are any of the decimals 0.3, 0.33, or 0.333 exactly $\frac{1}{3}$? Explain your reasoning.

C Find decimal equivalents for each group of fractions.

1. $-\frac{2}{5} \quad -\frac{3}{5} \quad -\frac{4}{5} \quad -\frac{6}{5}$ **2.** $\frac{2}{8} \quad \frac{3}{8} \quad \frac{4}{8} \quad \frac{5}{8} \quad \frac{6}{8} \quad \frac{7}{8}$ **3.** $\frac{1}{3} \quad \frac{2}{3} \quad \frac{3}{3} \quad \frac{4}{3}$

4. Describe the strategies you used to find decimal equivalents.

D Each number line below has two points labeled with decimal numbers and one with a question mark. In each case, what decimal number should go in place of the question mark?

1. 0.8 ? 0.9

2. 0.3 ↑↑ 0.35 ?

3. 0.8 ? 0.9

4. −0.9 ? −0.8

5. 0.499 ? 0.501

continued on the next page >

Problem **3.4** *continued*

E **1.** Write the decimal equivalent for each fraction.

$$-\frac{1}{2} \quad \frac{1}{3} \quad -\frac{1}{4} \quad \frac{1}{5} \quad \frac{1}{6} \quad -\frac{1}{8} \quad \frac{1}{10}$$

2. Draw a point for each decimal from part (1) on a number line.

3. How do the fractions $\frac{1}{4}$ and $\frac{1}{8}$ compare? How do the decimal equivalents of $-\frac{1}{4}$ and $-\frac{1}{8}$ compare?

4. How do the fractions $\frac{1}{3}$ and $\frac{1}{6}$ compare? How do the decimal equivalents of $-\frac{1}{3}$ and $-\frac{1}{6}$ compare?

5. Which fraction benchmark is closest to each of the following decimals?

    a. 0.18   **b.** −0.46   **c.** −0.225   **d.** 0.099

F Use your knowledge of fraction benchmarks and decimal place value to identify the greater number in each pair below. Use the greater than (>), less than (<), or equal to (=) symbols in writing your answers.

1. 0.1 and 0.9   **2.** 0.3 and 0.33   **3.** 0.25 and 0.250

4. 0.12 and 0.125   **5.** −0.1 and 0.1   **6.** −0.3 and −0.27

Choose three pairs of decimals from parts (1)–(6) to complete the following statements.

7. On the number line, __?__ is to the left of __?__ .

8. On the number line, __?__ is to the right of __?__ .

9. On the number line, __?__ and __?__ share the same point.

A C E Homework starts on page 82.

3.5 Earthquake Relief
Moving From Fractions to Decimals

On January 12, 2010, a 7.0-magnitude earthquake struck the country of Haiti. It destroyed many homes and caused major damage. Many people had no place to live and little clothing and food. In response, people from all over the world collected clothing, household items, and food to send to the victims of the earthquake.

Students at a middle school decided to collect food to distribute to families whose homes were destroyed. They packed what they collected into boxes to send to the families. The students had to solve some problems as they packed the boxes.

As you work on this problem, ask yourself

 When is decimal or fraction notation more useful, and why?

Problem 3.5

Each grade was assigned different numbers of families for which to pack boxes. Each grade shared the supplies equally among the families they were assigned. They had bags and plastic containers to repack items for the individual boxes. They also had a digital scale that measured in kilograms (kg) and grams (g).

A **1.** The sixth graders are packing six boxes. How much of each item should the students include in each box? Write your answer as a fraction and as a decimal.

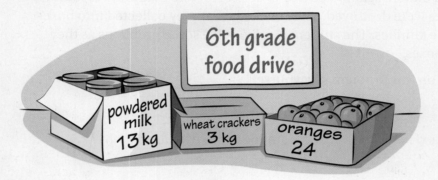

6th grade food drive

powdered milk 13 kg

wheat crackers 3 kg

oranges 24

2. Mary says that $\frac{13}{6}$ kg of milk goes in each box. Meleck says that $2\frac{1}{6}$ kg goes in, and he used his benchmark list to rewrite the amount as 2.16 kg. Funda says she divided the amount of milk by 6 and got 2.167 kg. With whom do you agree? Explain why.

3. Scooter said the ratio of numbers of oranges to boxes is 24 to 6. He calculated the number of oranges per box by writing *24 to 6*, then *4 to 1*. Is he correct? Explain.

Problem **3.5** *continued*

B The seventh graders are packing ten boxes. How much of each item should the students include in each box? Write your answer as a fraction and as a decimal.

7th grade food drive

peanut butter 23 kg

apples 45

cheddar cheese 8 kg

C The eighth graders are packing 14 boxes. How much of each item should the students include in each box? Write your answer as a fraction and as a decimal.

8th grade food drive

oranges 195

powdered milk 77 kg

peanut butter 39 kg

saltine crackers 24 kg

raisins 7 kg

swiss cheese 10.5 kg

D Describe your strategies for solving these problems.

ACE Homework starts on page 82.

Applications

1. Describe, in writing or with pictures, how $\frac{7}{3}$ compares to $2\frac{1}{3}$.

2. **Multiple Choice** On a number line from 0 to -10, where is $-\frac{13}{3}$ located?

    A. between 0 and -1 **B.** between -4 and -5

    C. between -5 and -6 **D.** between -6 and -7

3. Copy the number line below. Locate and label marks representing $2\frac{1}{4}$, $1\frac{9}{10}$, and $\frac{15}{4}$.

4. For parts (a)–(d), copy the number line below. Locate and label a point representing each fraction described.

    a. a fraction close to but greater than 1

    b. a fraction close to but less than -1

    c. a fraction close to but greater than $1\frac{1}{2}$

    d. a fraction close to but less than $-1\frac{1}{2}$

For Exercises 5–8, write each mixed number as an improper fraction.

5. $1\frac{2}{3}$ 6. $6\frac{3}{4}$ 7. $-9\frac{7}{9}$ 8. $-4\frac{2}{7}$

For Exercises 9–12, write each improper fraction as a mixed number.

9. $\frac{22}{4}$ 10. $\frac{10}{6}$ 11. $-\frac{17}{5}$ 12. $-\frac{36}{8}$

13. What numbers have an absolute value of $2\frac{1}{2}$?

14. What are some numbers that have an absolute value greater than $2\frac{1}{2}$?

15. A football team has four chances with the ball to gain ten yards and keep going to try to make a touchdown. A team gained 7 yards, lost 2, gained 4, and lost 1.

   a. How many total yards did the team move (forward or backward)?

   b. Did they gain enough to keep the ball? Explain your reasoning.

In many cold places, weather reports often include wind chills, the temperature of how cold it feels outside when you include the wind making it feel colder. For Exercises 16–19, write an inequality statement for the wind chills of the two locations.

16. Lincoln, NE compared to New Albin, IA   15°F ▓ 5°F

17. Viroqua, WI compared to Toledo, OH   −8°F ▓ 6°F

18. Minneapolis, MN compared to Duluth, MN   −10°F ▓ −25°F

19. Bozeman, MT compared to Rapid City, SD   −5°F ▓ −3°F

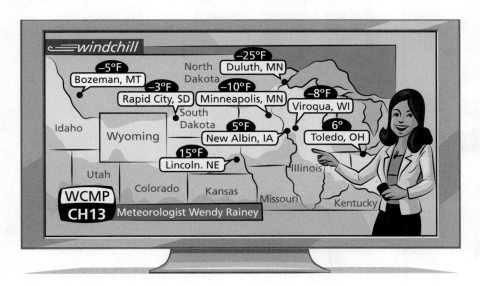

20. Mr. Bergman is having an end-of-the-year trivia contest. Each correct answer is worth 100 points, and each incorrect answer is worth −50 points. At the end of the contest Mr. Bergman is surprised by the final scores.

Blue Team	Orange Team	Purple Team
−50 points	−250 points	−200 points

The Blue team says they win because they have the highest score. The Orange team says that 250 is greater than 50, so they win. Which team should be called the winner? Explain.

21. Mrs. O'Brien's students are playing "The Ordering Game" as a whole class. A student draws five cards numbered −10 to 10. She rearranges the cards in different ways, and the class tries to figure out the reason for the order. In each of the orderings below, what reason was Ashley using for the order? Explain.

Ashley draws these cards.

a. Ordering #1

b. Ordering #2

c. Ordering #3

22. Use Ashley's three ordering methods from the previous problem to order the five cards that Herbert drew. Is there another ordering you could do that Ashley didn't show? Explain.

Herbert's Cards:

23. Franklin Middle School is having an end-of-the-year carnival with different games. One of the games is a bean-bag toss. The object is to get zero, or as close to zero as possible on the toss. Joseph's bag lands on an area labeled −3. Jeremiah's bag lands on an area labeled 2.

Joseph says, "I win because −3 < 2."

Jeremiah says, "No, we have to decide whose score is closer to zero. Since $|-3| = 3$ and $|2| = 2$, my score is closer to zero. I win."

Who is correct? Explain.

24. The elevation of different places on Earth is often given as the height above sea level, rounded to the nearest foot. Likewise, there are many places in the world whose elevation is below sea level. These are useful measurements because sea level is relatively constant across the planet.

City	Height above Sea Level
Indio, California	−20 feet
Denver, Colorado	5,280 feet
Wenzuan, China	16,700 feet
New Orleans, LA	−5 feet
Death Valley, California	−300 feet

a. Order the cities in the table from lowest elevation to highest elevation.

b. Order the cities from least to greatest distance from sea level.

c. Did you use absolute value in either part (a) or (b)? Explain.

As Rosemary works through some homework problems, she notices that negative numbers can often be rewritten using positive numbers if you change what you are talking about. For example, a golf score was given as −4 but Rosemary rewrote this as "4 shots under par." For Exercises 25–28, rewrite each negative situation using a positive value.

25. A savings account balance is −$15.00.

26. The elevation of a city is −20 feet.

27. A quarterback ran for −8 yards.

28. The amount of money a lemonade stand made on a rainy day was −$10.00.

For Exercises 29–40, compare each pair of fractions using benchmarks, number lines, and other strategies. Then use a less than (<), greater than (>), or equal to (=) symbol to complete each number sentence.

29. $\frac{8}{10}$ ■ $\frac{3}{8}$ **30.** $\frac{2}{3}$ ■ $\frac{4}{9}$ **31.** $\frac{3}{5}$ ■ $\frac{5}{12}$ **32.** $\frac{1}{3}$ ■ $\frac{2}{3}$

33. $\frac{3}{4}$ ■ $\frac{3}{5}$ **34.** $\frac{3}{2}$ ■ $-\frac{7}{6}$ **35.** $-\frac{8}{12}$ ■ $\frac{6}{9}$ **36.** $\frac{9}{10}$ ■ $\frac{10}{11}$

37. $-\frac{3}{12}$ ■ $-\frac{7}{12}$ **38.** $-\frac{5}{6}$ ■ $-\frac{5}{8}$ **39.** $-\frac{3}{7}$ ■ $-\frac{6}{14}$ **40.** $-\frac{4}{5}$ ■ $-\frac{7}{8}$

For Exercises 41–44, find a rational number between each pair of numbers.

41. $\frac{1}{8}$ and $\frac{1}{4}$ **42.** $\frac{1}{6}$ and $\frac{1}{12}$ **43.** $-\frac{1}{6}$ and $-\frac{2}{6}$ **44.** $-\frac{1}{4}$ and $\frac{2}{5}$

For Exercises 45–50, between which two benchmarks (of 0, $\frac{1}{2}$, 1, $1\frac{1}{2}$, and 2) does each fraction fall? Tell which is the nearer benchmark.

45. $\frac{3}{5}$ **46.** $1\frac{2}{6}$ **47.** $\frac{12}{10}$

48. $\frac{2}{18}$ **49.** $1\frac{8}{10}$ **50.** $1\frac{12}{15}$

51. Multiple Choice Which fraction is greatest?

   F. $\frac{7}{6}$ **G.** $\frac{9}{8}$ **H.** $\frac{13}{12}$ **J.** $\frac{14}{15}$

52. Multiple Choice Find the opposite of each number below. Which one is greatest?

   A. $\frac{7}{6}$ **B.** $\frac{9}{8}$ **C.** $\frac{13}{12}$ **D.** $\frac{14}{15}$

A pan of lasagna cut into 100 servings is equally shared among a group of people. For Exercises 53–55, determine the portion of the pan that each person receives given the number of people in each group. Write your answer as both a fractional and a decimal part of a pan.

53. 20 people   **54.** 40 people   **55.** 30 people

For Exercises 56–59, write a fraction equivalent to the decimal.

56. 0.08   **57.** 0.4   **58.** -0.04 **59.** -0.84

For Exercises 60–63, write a decimal equivalent to the fraction.

60. $\frac{3}{4}$ **61.** $\frac{7}{50}$ **62.** $-\frac{13}{25}$ **63.** $-\frac{7}{10}$

64. Which is greater, forty-five hundredths or six tenths? Explain. Draw a picture if it helps you explain.

65. Which is greater, 0.6 or 0.60? Explain. Draw a picture if it helps you explain.

For Exercises 66–68, a full one-hundredths grid represents the number 1. What fraction and decimal is represented by each of the shaded parts?

66.

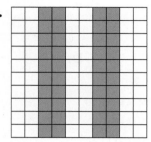

67.

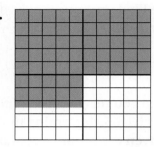

68.

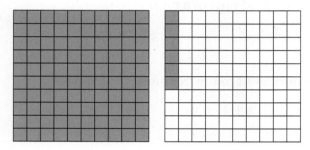

69. Name three fractions whose decimal equivalent is 0.40. Explain how you know each fraction is equivalent to 0.40. Draw a picture if it helps you explain.

For Exercises 70–72, copy the part of the number line given. Then find the "step" by determining the difference from one mark to another. Label the unlabeled marks with decimal numbers.

Sample:

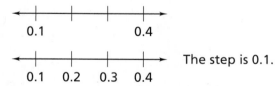

The step is 0.1.

70.

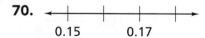

71.

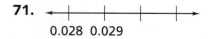

72.

For Exercises 73–76, give the fraction listed that is nearest on the number line to that decimal.

$$-\frac{1}{2} \quad -\frac{1}{3} \quad -\frac{1}{4} \quad -\frac{1}{5} \quad -\frac{1}{6} \quad -\frac{1}{8} \quad -\frac{1}{10}$$

73. −0.30   **74.** −0.50   **75.** −0.12333   **76.** −0.15

For Exercises 77–82, copy each pair of numbers. Insert <, >, or = to make a true statement.

77. 0.205 ▨ 0.21   **78.** 0.1 ▨ 0.1000

79. −0.04 ▨ −0.050   **80.** −1.03 ▨ −0.03

81. $\frac{5}{10}$ ▨ 0.6   **82.** $-\frac{3}{5}$ ▨ −0.3

For Exercises 83 and 84, rewrite the numbers in order from least to greatest.

83. 0.33, −0.12, −0.127, 0.2, $\frac{45}{10}$

84. $-\frac{45}{10}$, $\frac{3}{1000}$, −0.005, 0.34

85. Multiple Choice The orchestra at Johnson School is responsible for cleaning up a 15-mile section of highway. There are 45 students in the orchestra. If each orchestra member cleans the same-size section, which of the decimals indicates the part of a mile cleaned by each student?

F. 0.25   **G.** 0.33   **H.** 0.333...   **J.** 0.5

86. Pilar divided 1 by 9 on her calculator and found that $\frac{1}{9}$ was approximately 0.1111. Find decimal approximations for each of the following fractions.

   a. $\frac{2}{9}$ **b.** $\frac{11}{9}$ **c.** $\frac{6}{9}$ **d.** $\frac{2}{3}$

   e. Describe any patterns that you see.

87. Belinda used her calculator to find the decimal equivalent of the fraction $\frac{21}{28}$. When she entered 21 ÷ 28, the calculator gave an answer that looked familiar. Why do you think she recognized it?

88. Suppose a new student starts school today and your teacher asks you to teach her how to find decimal equivalents for fractions. What would you tell her? How would you convince the student that your method works?

Connections

For Exercises 89–91, use the following information. Each student activity group at Johnson School agreed to pick up litter along a ten-mile stretch of highway. Draw number lines to show your reasoning.

89. Kelly and Sean work together to clean a section of highway that is $\frac{10}{3}$ miles long. Write this distance as a mixed number.

90. The Drama Club's stretch of highway is very hilly and full of trash. They can clean $1\frac{2}{3}$ miles each day. Jacqueline says that in four days, they will be able to clean $\frac{19}{3}$ miles. Is she correct? Explain.

91. The Chess Club is cleaning a very littered section of highway. Each day the members clean $1\frac{3}{4}$ miles of highway. After four days of hard work, Lakeisha says they have cleaned $\frac{28}{4}$ miles of highway. Glenda says they have cleaned 7 miles of roadway. Who is right? Why?

92. Ten students went to a pizza parlor together. They ordered eight small pizzas.

    a. How much pizza will each student get if they share the pizzas equally? Express your answer as a fraction and as a decimal.

    b. Explain how you thought about the problem. Draw a picture that would convince someone that your answer is correct.

93. If you look through a microscope that makes objects appear ten times larger, 1 centimeter (cm) on a metric ruler looks like this:

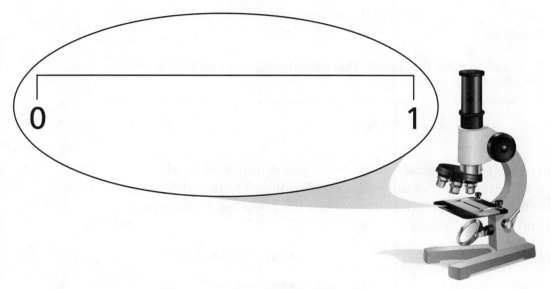

    a. Copy this microscope's view of 1 cm. Divide the length for 1 cm into ten equal parts. What fraction of the "centimeter" does each of these parts represent?

    b. Now think about dividing one of these smaller parts into ten equal parts. What part of the original "centimeter" does each of the new segments represent?

    c. If you were to divide one of these new small parts into ten parts again, what part of the original "centimeter" would each of the new small parts represent?

Extensions

For Exercises 94–96, find every fraction with a denominator less than 50 that is equivalent to the given fraction.

94. $\frac{3}{15}$

95. $\frac{8}{3}$

96. $1\frac{4}{6}$

97. Find five fractions between $-\frac{8}{10}$ and $-\frac{4}{5}$.

98. Does $\frac{4}{5}$, $\frac{17}{23}$, or $\frac{51}{68}$ represent the greatest part of a whole? Explain your reasoning.

99. Copy the number line below. Place and label marks for 0, $\frac{3}{4}$, $\frac{1}{8}$, and $2\frac{2}{3}$.

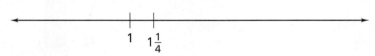

For Exercises 100–105, find an estimate if you cannot find an exact answer. You may find that drawing a number line, a hundredths grid, or some other diagram is useful in solving the problem. Explain your reasoning for each problem.

100. What is $\frac{1}{4}$ of 12?

101. What is $\frac{3}{4}$ of 8?

102. What is $\frac{2}{9}$ of 3?

103. What is $\frac{2}{9}$ of 18?

104. What is $\frac{1}{4}$ of 3?

105. What is $\frac{3}{4}$ of 3?

Mathematical Reflections 3

In your work in this Investigation, you used number lines to investigate relationships among fractions and decimals and to estimate the size of a number. These questions will help you summarize what you have learned.

Think about your answers to these questions. Discuss your ideas with other students and your teacher. Then write a summary of your findings in your notebook.

1. **a.** Not every fraction refers to a quantity between 0 and 1. Give some examples of numbers that are greater than 1 or less than 0.

   b. How is a number and its opposite represented on a number line? Give examples.

2. **a. What** are some strategies for deciding which of two numbers is greater? Give examples.

   b. When comparing two positive whole numbers with different numbers of digits, such as 115 and 37, the one with more digits is greater. Does this rule work for comparing decimals?

Common Core Mathematical Practices

As you worked on the Problems in this Investigation, you used prior knowledge to make sense of the Problems. You also applied Mathematical Practices to solve the Problems. Think back over your work, the ways you thought about the Problems, and how you used Mathematical Practices.

Elena described her thoughts in the following way:

> We thought that Blake was correct in his reasoning in Problem 3.2. He claimed that if the absolute value of a number is larger than the absolute value of another number then the first number is further from zero. We tried lots of numbers and they all satisfied this claim.
>
> Then we noticed that we did not try a positive and a negative number. For example, the absolute value of $-\frac{3}{4}$ is greater than the absolute value of $\frac{1}{2}$ but even though $-\frac{3}{4}$ is not greater than $\frac{1}{2}$, $-\frac{3}{4}$ is still further from 0 than $\frac{1}{2}$.
>
> Blake's conjecture is true.

Common Core Standards for Mathematical Practice

MP3 Construct viable arguments and critique the reasoning of others

- What other Mathematical Practices can you identify in Elena's reasoning?

- Describe a Mathematical Practice that you and your classmates used to solve a different Problem in this Investigation.

Investigation 4

Working With Percents

In this Unit, you have represented quantities as fractions and ratios to answer the questions "How much?" or "How many?" or "Which is better?" When you use a ratio to answer a question, you are making a comparison.

When school construction projects are proposed, voters often must agree on a tax increase to pay for the project. Voters in two neighborhoods were surveyed and asked, "Would you vote *yes* for the construction of a new school gym?" The table shows the results of the survey. Decide which neighborhood is more enthusiastic about building a new school gym.

Neighborhood	Yes	No
Whitehills	31	69
Bailey	17	33

One way to compare the two neighborhoods is to figure out what the numbers in each neighborhood would be if 100 people were surveyed and the rate of support stayed the same. Fractions with 100 in the denominator are useful. You can easily order them and write them as decimals.

....

Common Core State Standards

6.RP.A.2 Understand the concept of a unit rate *a/b* associated with a ratio *a : b* with *b* ≠ 0, and use rate language in the context of a ratio relationship.

6.RP.A.3c Find a percent of a quantity as a rate per 100 (e.g., 30% of a quantity means $\frac{30}{100}$ times the quantity); solve problems involving finding the whole, given a part and the percent.

6.RP.A.3d Use ratio reasoning to convert measurement units; manipulate and transform units appropriately when multiplying or dividing quantities.

Also 6.RP.A.1, 6.RP.A.3, 6.RP.A.3b, 6.NS.B.2

Another useful way to express a fraction with a denominator of 100 is to use the percent symbol. A **percent** is a part-to-whole comparison that uses 100 as the whole. The word *percent* means "out of 100." For example, 8% means 8 of 100, or $\frac{8}{100}$, or 8 per 100.

In this Investigation, you will use percents, fractions, and decimals to express relationships and make comparisons. You will develop strategies for estimating and finding percentages equivalent to fractions and ratios.

In Investigation 1, you found the fraction of a fundraising goal each grade achieved. The thermometers could have been marked with percents instead of fractions of the goal to express the same amount.

- What fractions match each of the marked percent values on these thermometers?

- What dollar amounts match each of the marked percent values on these thermometers?

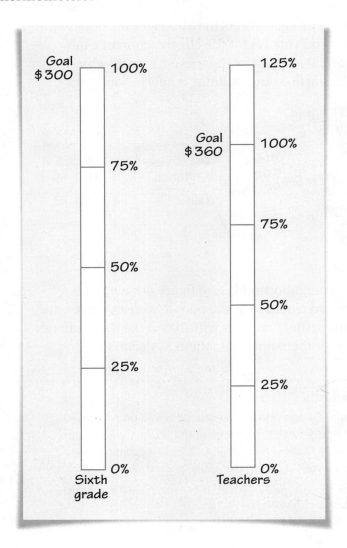

4.1 Who Is the Best?
Making Sense of Percents

Sports statistics are often given in percents. An important statistic for basketball teams is the successful free-throw percent. You will use mathematics to compare the basketball statistics of two well-known men's basketball teams in the National Collegiate Athletic Association (NCAA).

- How are free-throw shooting averages determined for basketball teams?

Problem 4.1

During a recent year, two NCAA basketball teams made 108 out of 126 free-throw attempts and 195 out of 257 attempts. It is difficult to tell which team was better at free throws that year using raw numbers. Therefore, sports announcers often give percents instead of raw numbers.

A Will drew pictures similar to the fund-raising thermometers to help him think about the percent of free throws made by the two teams. Then he got stuck! Help Will use the pictures he drew to decide which team is better at free throws.

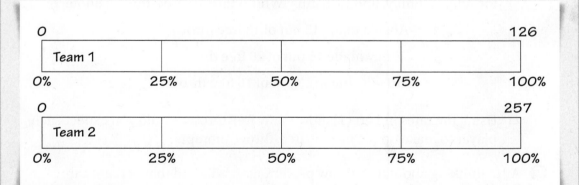

1. For each bar, estimate the number of free throws that should go with each marked percent in the picture.

2. For each team, shade the percent bar to show how many free throws the team made and estimate that percentage. Explain how you did this.

3. At this rate, how many free throws would you expect Team 1 to make in their next 200 free-throw attempts? How many would you expect Team 2 to make in their next 200 free-throw attempts?

continued on the next page >

Problem 4.1 *continued*

B Alisha said that she could get better estimates of each team's free-throw percentage using the percent bars below. Copy and complete her percent bars to estimate each team's free-throw percentage. Compare your answers to your answers for Question A.

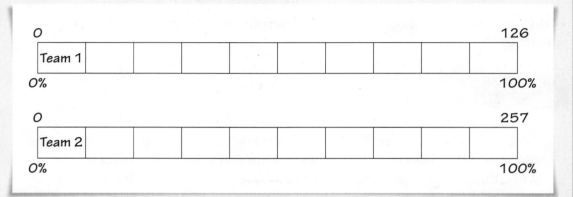

C Will, in Question A, and Alisha, in Question B, each use percent bars to show common percent benchmarks. What benchmarks does each student use?

D 1. Use percent bars and your own ideas to estimate free-throw percentages for Angela, Emily, and Christina. Who is the best free-throw shooter?

Angela made 12 out of 15 free throws

Emily made 15 out of 20 free throws

Christina made 13 out of 16 free throws

2. Using the rates in part (1), how many free throws would you expect each player to make on the next 30 free-throw attempts?

E After thinking about free-throw percentages, Will said that percents are like fractions. Alisha disagreed and said that percents are more like ratios. Do you agree more with Will or with Alisha? Explain.

A C E Homework starts on page 103.

4.2 Genetic Traits
Finding Percents

Have you ever heard of *genes*? (Not the "jeans" you wear, even though they sound the same.) What color are your eyes? Is your hair curly? Are your earlobes attached? You are born with a unique set of genes that help to determine these traits.

Scientists who study human traits such as eye and hair color are *geneticists*. Geneticists are interested in how common certain human traits are.

Look at the earlobe of a classmate. Is it attached or detached? The type of earlobe you have is a trait determined partly by your genes. Here is a description of four genetic traits:

- A widow's peak is a V-shaped hairline.

- A dimple is a small indentation, usually near the mouth.

- Straight hair does not have natural waves or curls.

- An earlobe is attached if its lowest point is attached directly to the head.

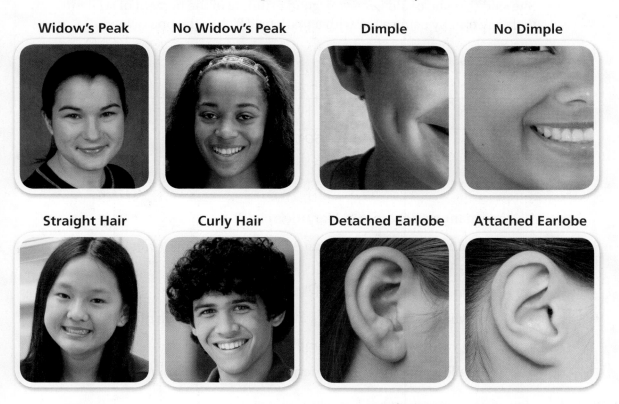

Widow's Peak	No Widow's Peak	Dimple	No Dimple

Straight Hair	Curly Hair	Detached Earlobe	Attached Earlobe

Problem 4.2

A 1. Copy and complete the table of genetic traits below.

**Traits Observed in a Middle
School Classroom**

Trait	Yes	No	Total
Attached Earlobes	12	■	30
Dimples	7	■	30
Straight Hair	24	■	30
Widow's Peak	17	■	30

2. For each trait, use a percent bar or another strategy to estimate the percent of people in the class who have that trait.

3. Using the percents from part (2) as rates, how many people in a school of 500 are likely to have a widow's peak?

B Marjorie wanted to find the percent of students in her class with dimples. She said that she could get a very good estimate of the percent of students with any trait by using a bar with a mark for 1% like the one below.

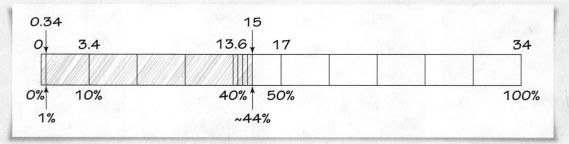

1. How many students are in Marjorie's class?

2. How did Marjorie figure out that 3.4 is at the 10% mark and 13.6 is at the 40% mark?

3. How many students in Marjorie's class have dimples?

4. About what percent of students in Marjorie's class have dimples?

5. How do you think Marjorie found that percent?

6. Are dimples more common in Marjorie's class than in your class? Explain.

C How is using a percent bar like using a rate table?

A C E Homework starts on page 103.

4.3 The Art of Comparison
Using Ratios and Percents

Do you have a favorite work of art? Is it by a famous artist such as Claude Monet, Georgia O'Keefe, or is it by your little sister?

Art museums own more pieces than they can display at one time. This means that art must be stored when it is not hanging in a gallery. A museum curator chooses which works to exhibit.

The Walker Art Center in Minneapolis, Minnesota held an exhibit entitled $\frac{50}{50}$. For the exhibit, the public voted via the Internet on which pieces they wanted the museum to display, and curators chose the remaining pieces.

- What do you think $\frac{50}{50}$ refers to in the title?

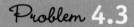

Problem 4.3

Another art museum held a similar $\frac{50}{50}$ exhibit. The picture shows the public's part of the exhibit. The curators' part is covered up.

A How many works of art do you estimate were in the exhibit? Is there any other information that would help you make a better estimate? Explain.

continued on the next page >

Problem 4.3 continued

B Below is a picture of the complete exhibit. How does this picture change your estimate from Question A?

C The picture in Question B shows you about $\frac{2}{3}$ of each part of the exhibit.

1. Make a drawing to show the size of the whole exhibit.

2. Use your drawing to estimate the number of works in each part.

D **1.** Estimate the percent of the exhibit chosen by the public. Estimate the percent chosen by curators.

2. Use the percents from part (1). If there were 200 pieces in the exhibit, how many artworks do you think the public chose? How many do you think the curators chose?

E What title would you choose for this exhibit using percents and ratios?

A C E Homework starts on page 103.

Applications

1. In a recent year, Team 1 made 191 out of 238 free-throw attempts and Team 2 made 106 out of 160 free-throw attempts. Copy and use the percent bars to answer each question.

a. What fraction benchmark is close to the number of free throws made by each team?

b. Estimate the percent of free throws made by each team in the season.

c. If Team 1's free-throw rate does not change, how many free throws will Team 1 make in the next 200 throws? How many free throws will Team 1 make in the next 20 throws?

2. **Multiple Choice** Choose the best score on a quiz.

   A. 15 points out of 25

   B. 8 points out of 14

   C. 25 points out of 45

   D. 27 points out of 50

3. **Multiple Choice** Choose the best score on a quiz.

   F. 150 points out of 250

   G. 24 points out of 42

   H. 75 points out of 135

   J. 75 points out of 150

4. **Multiple Choice** What is the correct percent for a quiz score of 14 points out of 20?

   A. 43%   B. 53%   C. 70%   D. 75%

5. **Multiple Choice** What is the correct percent for a quiz score of 26 points out of 60?

   F. about 43%   G. about 57%   H. about 68%   J. about 76%

For Exercises 6–14, use the data in the table below.

Distribution of Cat Weights

Weight (lb)	Males		Females	
	Kitten	Adult	Kitten	Adult
0–5.9	8	1	7	4
6–10.9	0	16	0	31
11–15.9	2	15	0	10
16–20	0	4	0	2
Total	10	36	7	47

1.75 lb

6. **a.** What fraction of the cats are female?

   b. What fraction of the cats are male?

   c. Write each fraction as a decimal and as a percent.

7. **a.** What fraction of the cats are kittens?

   b. What fraction of the cats are adults?

   c. Write each fraction as a decimal and a percent.

8. **a.** What fraction of the kittens are male?

   b. Write the fraction as a decimal and as a percent.

9. What percent of the cats weigh between 11 and 15.9 pounds?

10. What percent of the cats weigh between 0 and 5.9 pounds?

11. What percent of the cats are male kittens and weigh between 11 and 15.9 pounds?

12. What percent of the cats are female and weigh between 6 and 15.9 pounds?

13. What percent of the cats are kittens and weigh between 16 and 20 pounds?

14. What percent of the female cats weigh between 0 and 5.9 pounds?

For Exercises 15–18, use the following information: In a recent survey, 150 dog owners and 200 cat owners were asked what type of food their pets liked. Here are the results of the survey.

Pet Food Preferences

Preference	Dogs	Cats
Human Food Only	75	36
Pet Food Only	45	116
Human and Pet Food	30	48

15. Find the category of food most favored by dogs (Human, Pet, or Human and Pet). Write the data from this category as a fraction, as a decimal, and as a percent of the total dog owners surveyed.

16. Find the category of food most favored by cats. Write the data from this category as a fraction, as a decimal, and as a percent of the total cat owners surveyed.

17. Suppose only 100 dog owners were surveyed with similar results. Estimate the counts in each of the three food categories.

18. Suppose 50 cat owners were surveyed with similar results. Estimate the counts in each of the three food categories.

19. Elisa's math test score, with extra credit included, was $\frac{26}{25}$. What percent is this?

20. Use the data below. Which neighborhood, Elmhurst or Little Neck, is more in favor of building a new sports complex? Explain your reasoning.

Votes on a New Sports Complex

Neighborhood	Yes	No
Elmhurst	43	57
Little Neck	41	9

21. In Problem 4.1, you found free-throw percentages for Angela, Emily, and Christina. Write each girl's free-throw success as a ratio of *percent made* : *percent missed*.

Angela made 12 out of 15 free throws

Emily made 15 out of 20 free throws

Christina made 13 out of 16 free throws

22. A candy manufacturer says on its Web site that it wants to reach a 60 : 40 consumer taste preference for new products. What do you think this means?

23. In some cars, the rear seat folds down to add more space in the trunk. Often, there is a 60 : 40 split in the rear seat instead of 50 : 50. If a rear seat is 60 inches wide with a 60 : 40 split, how wide are the two parts?

24. The 90 : 10 rule says that part of your success in life comes from what happens to you and part comes from how you react to it. Which is 90 and which is 10? Explain.

25. Copy the table and fill in the missing parts.

Percent	Decimal	Fraction
62%	■	■
■	■	$\frac{4}{9}$
■	1.23	■
■	■	$\frac{12}{15}$
■	2.65	■
■	0.55	■
48%	■	■
■	■	$\frac{12}{10}$

Connections

Compare each pair of fractions in Exercises 26–31 using benchmarks or another strategy that makes sense to you. Copy the fractions and insert <, >, or = to make a true statement.

26. $\frac{7}{10}$ ■ $\frac{5}{8}$

27. $\frac{11}{12}$ ■ $\frac{12}{13}$

28. $\frac{12}{15}$ ■ $\frac{12}{14}$

29. $\frac{3}{8}$ ■ $\frac{4}{8}$

30. $\frac{3}{5}$ ■ $\frac{4}{6}$

31. $\frac{4}{3}$ ■ $\frac{15}{12}$

32. Copy the table below and fill in the missing parts.

Fraction	Mixed Number
$\frac{13}{5}$	■
■	$5\frac{2}{7}$
■	$9\frac{3}{4}$
$\frac{23}{3}$	■

33. The following percents are a good set of benchmarks because they have common fraction and decimal equivalents. Copy the table and fill in the missing parts. Use your table to learn these equivalents.

Percent	10%	$12\frac{1}{2}$%	20%	25%	30%	$33\frac{1}{3}$%	50%	$66\frac{2}{3}$%	75%
Fraction	■	■	■	■	■	■	■	■	■
Decimal	■	■	■	■	■	■	■	■	■

Extensions

In Exercises 34–36, determine what fraction is the correct label for the mark halfway between the two marked values on the number line. Write the fraction as a percent and as a decimal.

34.

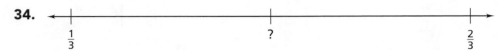

35.

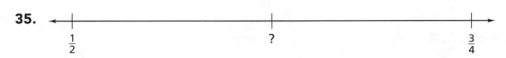

36.

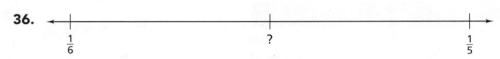

37. What fraction of the square below is shaded? Explain.

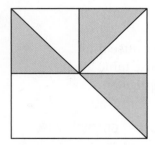

38. In decimal form, what part of the square below is shaded? Explain.

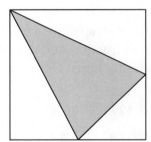

39. What percent of the square below is shaded? Explain.

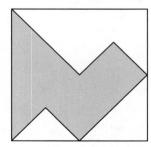

40. A pet store sells digestible mouthwash for cats. To promote the new product, the store is offering $.50 off the regular price of $2.00 for an 8-ounce bottle. What is the percent discount on the mouthwash?

In each of Exercises 41–43, what percent is halfway between the two percents labeled on the percent bar? What number is represented by the percent?

41.

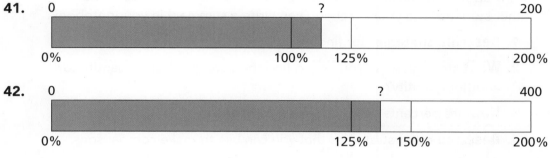

42.

43.

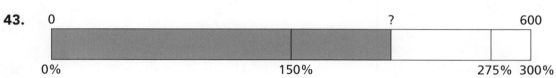

44. A store offers a discount of 30% on all reference books.

a. If a dictionary costs $12 before the discount, what is the dollar amount of the discount?

b. If a book on insect identification originally costs $15, how much will you have to pay for it?

c. If you pay $14 for a math dictionary, what was the original price of the dictionary?

Did You Know?
....

In the 1400s, the phrase "per cento" stood for "per 100." Writing "per cento" over and over again probably got tiresome. Manuscripts on arithmetic from about 1650 show that people began to replace "per cento" with "per $\frac{0}{0}$" or "p $\frac{0}{0}$." Later, the "per" was dropped and the symbol $\frac{0}{0}$ appeared alone. Then, over time, $\frac{0}{0}$ became %, the symbol used today.

In this Investigation, you used percent bars, ratios, and fraction reasoning to investigate percents. These questions will help you summarize what you have learned.

Think about your answers to these questions. Discuss your ideas with other students and your teacher. Then write a summary in your notebook.

1. **Describe** strategies for finding a percent of a known quantity.

2. **What** strategies can you use to find the percent of one quantity to another quantity?

3. **How** are percents used to make a comparison?

4. **Describe** other strategies that you can use to make comparisons.

Common Core Mathematical Practices

As you worked on the Problems in this Investigation, you used prior knowledge to make sense of the Problems. You also applied Mathematical Practices to solve the Problems. Think back over your work, the ways you thought about the Problems, and how you used Mathematical Practices.

Ken described his thoughts in the following way:

> In Problem 4.2, we talked about how we could find certain common traits in various populations of people.
>
> We used percent bars and rate tables to estimate the percent of people in a class who responded to a survey asking who has attached earlobes, dimples, straight hair, and a widow's peak.
>
> We analyzed the relationships with percent bars and rate tables and drew conclusions based on our representations. We compared the methods. Since the numbers did not quickly scale up to 100, some of us preferred to use the percent bar or division to find the percentage.

Common Core Standards for Mathematical Practice
MP5 Use appropriate tools strategically

- What other Mathematical Practices can you identify in Ken's reasoning?

- Describe a Mathematical Practice that you and your classmates used to solve a different Problem in this Investigation.

In this Unit, you extended your knowledge of fractions, ratios, decimals, and percents. You learned how to

- Use ratios and fractions to make comparisons
- Relate fractions and decimals to their locations on a number line
- Relate fractions, decimals, ratios, and percents to each other
- Compare and order fractions and decimals
- Identify and produce equivalent fractions, decimals, and percents
- Identify and produce equivalent ratios, rate tables, and unit rates

Use Your Understanding: Number Sense

Test your understanding of and skill working with fractions, decimals, and percents by solving the following problems.

1. The diagram shows a puzzle made up of familiar shapes.

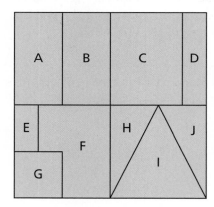

a. What fraction of the puzzle does each piece cover? Use your measurement estimation skills and reasoning to find each fraction.

b. Find two puzzle pieces with sizes in the ratio 2 : 1. Is there more than one possible answer? Explain.

c. What is the ratio of the size of piece C to the size of piece H?

2. Jose draws eight cards from a deck of number cards. He shows the position of each number on a number line as a fraction, as a decimal, and as a percent of the distance between 0 and 1.

The number line below shows the fraction $\frac{1}{4}$ along with its corresponding decimal and percent.

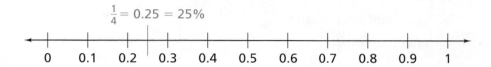

   a. Copy the number line and show the position of each of the other numbers.

   b. Label each position as a fraction, a decimal, and a percent of the distance between 0 and 1.

Explain Your Reasoning

You have explored relationships among ratios, fractions, decimals, and percents in many different problems. You have learned strategies for working with fractions, decimals, and percents that apply in any situation.

3. Describe a strategy that you can use to compare each pair of numbers.

   a. $\frac{5}{8}$ and $\frac{7}{8}$ **b.** $\frac{3}{4}$ and $\frac{3}{5}$ **c.** $\frac{3}{4}$ and $\frac{5}{8}$

   d. $\frac{3}{8}$ and $\frac{2}{3}$ **e.** $\frac{3}{4}$ and $\frac{4}{5}$ **f.** $\frac{2}{3}$ and $\frac{5}{8}$

For Exercises 4–6, find each number. Then describe the strategy that you used.

4. **a.** a fraction equivalent to $\frac{16}{20}$

    b. a decimal equivalent to $\frac{16}{20}$

    c. a percent for $\frac{16}{20}$

5. **a.** a decimal equivalent to 0.18

    b. a fraction equivalent to 0.18

    c. a percent for 0.18

6. **a.** a fraction for 35%

    b. a decimal for 35%

7. A square is shaded so that the ratio of the size of the shaded part to the size of the unshaded part is 3 : 1. Describe a strategy that you can use to find the fraction of the square that is shaded.

8. Two thirds of the students in a sixth-grade class wear glasses. Describe a strategy that you can use to find the ratio of the number of students who wear glasses to the number of students who do not wear glasses.

9. To make chocolate milk, a recipe calls for 12 tablespoons of chocolate syrup for 4 cups of milk. Describe a strategy for finding the amount of chocolate syrup needed to make each quantity of chocolate milk.

    a. 1 cup

    b. 20 cups

English / Spanish Glossary

A **absolute value** The absolute value of a number is its distance from 0 on the number line. Numbers that are the same distance from 0 have the same absolute value.

valor absoluto El valor absoluto de un número es su distancia del 0 en una recta numérica. Se puede interpretar como el valor de un número cuando no importa su signo. Por ejemplo, tanto -3 como 3 tienen un valor absoluto de 3.

B **base ten numeration** The common system of writing whole numbers and decimal fractions using digits 0, 1, 2, 3, 4, 5, 6, 7, 8, and 9 and place values that are powers of 10. For example, the base ten numeral 5620.301 represents $5000 + 600 + 20 + 0 + \frac{3}{10} + \frac{0}{100} + \frac{1}{1000}$.

numeración en base diez Un sistema común de escritura de números enteros y fracciones decimales que usa los dígitos 0, 1, 2, 3, 4, 5, 6, 7, 8 y 9, y valores de posición que son potencias de 10. Por ejemplo, el número de base diez 5620.301 representa $5000 + 600 + 20 + 0 + \frac{3}{10} + \frac{0}{100} + \frac{1}{1000}$.

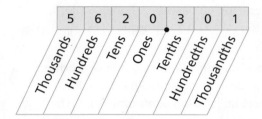

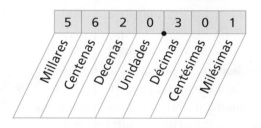

benchmark A reference number that can be used to estimate the size of other numbers. For work with fractions, 0, $\frac{1}{2}$, and 1 are good benchmarks. We often estimate fractions or decimals with benchmarks because it is easier to do arithmetic with them, and estimates often give enough accuracy for the situation. For example, many fractions and decimals—such as $\frac{37}{50}$, $\frac{5}{8}$, 0.43, and 0.55—can be thought of as being close to $\frac{1}{2}$. You might say $\frac{5}{8}$ is between $\frac{1}{2}$ and 1 but closer to $\frac{1}{2}$, so you can estimate $\frac{5}{8}$ to be about $\frac{1}{2}$. We also use benchmarks to help compare fractions and decimals. For example, we could say that $\frac{5}{8}$ is greater than 0.43 because $\frac{5}{8}$ is greater than $\frac{1}{2}$ and 0.43 is less than $\frac{1}{2}$.

punto de referencia Un número que se puede usar como referencia para estimar la magnitud de otros números. Los números 0, $\frac{1}{2}$ y 1 son puntos de referencia convenientes para el trabajo con fracciones. Con frecuencia, estimamos fracciones o números decimales usando puntos de referencia porque resulta más fácil hacer cálculos aritméticos con ellos, y las estimaciones suelen ser lo suficientemente precisas para la situación. Por ejemplo, muchas fracciones y números decimales, como $\frac{37}{50}$, $\frac{5}{8}$, 0.43 y 0.55, se pueden considerar cercanos a $\frac{1}{2}$. Se puede decir que $\frac{5}{8}$ está entre $\frac{1}{2}$ y 1, pero más cerca de $\frac{1}{2}$, por lo que se puede estimar que $\frac{5}{8}$ es aproximadamente $\frac{1}{2}$. También usamos puntos de referencia como ayuda para comparar fracciones y números decimales. Por ejemplo, podemos decir que $\frac{5}{8}$ es mayor que 0.43, porque $\frac{5}{8}$ es mayor que $\frac{1}{2}$ y 0.43 es menor que $\frac{1}{2}$.

C compare Academic Vocabulary To tell or show how two things are alike and different.

related terms: *analyze, relate*

sample Compare the fractions $\frac{2}{3}$ and $\frac{3}{8}$.

I set the fractions strips representing $\frac{2}{3}$ and $\frac{3}{8}$ next to each other to see which fraction was greater. $\frac{2}{3} > \frac{3}{8}$

comparar Vocabulario académico Decir o mostrar en qué se parecen y en qué se diferencian dos cosas.

términos relacionados: *analizar, relacionar*

ejemplo Compara las fracciones $\frac{2}{3}$ y $\frac{3}{8}$.

Coloco las tiras de fracciones que representan $\frac{2}{3}$ y $\frac{3}{8}$ una junto a la otra para ver cuál fracción es mayor. $\frac{2}{3} > \frac{3}{8}$

D decimal a fraction written in base ten numeration. For example, the fraction $\frac{375}{1000} = 0.375$ because $= + \frac{7}{100} + \frac{5}{1000}$.

número decimal Una fracción escrita con numeración en base diez. Por ejemplo, la fracción $\frac{375}{1000} = 0.375$ porque $= + \frac{7}{100} + \frac{5}{1000}$.

denominator The number written below the line in a fraction. In the fraction $\frac{3}{4}$, 4 is the denominator. In the part-whole interpretation of fractions, the denominator shows the number of equal-size parts into which the whole has been split.

denominador El número que se escribe debajo de la línea en una fracción. En la fracción $\frac{3}{4}$, 4 es el denominador. En la interpretación de partes y enteros al hablar de fracciones, el denominador muestra el número de partes de igual tamaño en que se divide el entero.

describe Academic Vocabulary To explain or tell in detail. A written description can contain facts and other information needed to communicate your answer. A diagram or a graph may also be included.

related terms: *express, explain, illustrate*

sample Describe in writing or with pictures how $\frac{5}{4}$ compares to $1\frac{1}{4}$.

I can use fraction strips divided into fourths to show that $1\frac{1}{4}$ is equal to $\frac{5}{4}$.

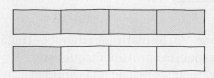

I can also compare using division. 5 divided by 4 is 1 remainder 1. So $\frac{5}{4}$ is the same as $1\frac{5}{4}$.

describir Vocabulario académico Explicar o decir con detalle. Una descripción escrita puede contener datos y otra información necesaria para comunicar tu respuesta. También se puede incluir un diagrama o una gráfica.

términos relacionados: *expresar, explicar, ilustrar*

ejemplo Describe por escrito o mediante un dibujo en qué se parecen o en qué se diferencian $\frac{5}{4}$ y $1\frac{1}{4}$.

Puedo usar tiras de fracciones divididas en cuartos para mostrar que $1\frac{1}{4}$ es igual a $\frac{5}{4}$.

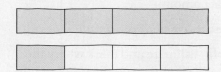

También puedo comparar usando la división. 5 dividido entre 4 es 1 con un residuo de 1. Así, $\frac{5}{4}$ es lo mismo que $1\frac{1}{4}$.

E **equivalent fractions** Fractions that are equal in value, but may have different numerators and denominators. For example, $\frac{2}{3}$ and $\frac{14}{21}$ are equivalent fractions. The shaded part of this rectangle represents both $\frac{2}{3}$ and $\frac{14}{21}$.

fracciones equivalentes Fracciones de igual valor que pueden tener diferentes numeradores y denominadores. Por ejemplo, $\frac{2}{3}$ y $\frac{14}{21}$ son fracciones equivalentes. La parte coloreada de este rectángulo representa tanto $\frac{2}{3}$ como $\frac{14}{21}$.

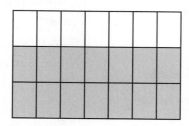

estimate Academic Vocabulary To find an approximate answer that is relatively close to an exact amount.

related terms: *approximate, guess*

sample Estimate and mark where the number 2 should be on the number line below. Explain.

estimar Vocabulario académico Hallar una respuesta aproximada que esté relativamente cerca de una cantidad exacta.

términos relacionados: *aproximar, suponer*

ejemplo Haz una estimación y marca dónde debe estar el número 2 en la recta numérica siguiente. Explica tu respuesta.

Since $1\frac{1}{5}$ is the same as $\frac{6}{5}$, I divided the space between 0 and $1\frac{1}{5}$ into six parts. This gives me an idea of the length of $\frac{1}{5}$.

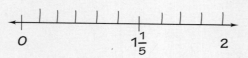

Then I added 4 marks after $1\frac{1}{5}$ to estimate where $1\frac{5}{5}$, or 2, should be on the number line.

Puesto que $1\frac{1}{5}$ es lo mismo que $\frac{6}{5}$, divido el espacio entre 0 y $1\frac{1}{5}$ en cinco partes. Esto me da una idea de la longitud de $\frac{1}{5}$.

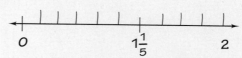

Luego agrego 4 marcas después de $1\frac{1}{5}$ para estimar donde debería estar $1\frac{5}{5}$, ó 2, en la recta numérica.

explain Academic Vocabulary To give facts and details that make an idea easier to understand. Explaining can involve a written summary supported by a diagram, chart, table, or a combination of these.

related terms: *analyze, clarify, describe, justify, tell*

sample Explain why $\frac{9}{10}$ is greater than $\frac{7}{8}$.

> I can write the fractions in decimal form and compare digits.
>
> | $\frac{9}{10}$ | 0.900 |
> |---|---|
> | $\frac{7}{8}$ | 0.875 |
>
> Because 9 in the tenths place is greater than 8, $\frac{9}{10}$ is greater than $\frac{7}{8}$.
> I can also write equivalent fractions with a common denominator and compare the numerators. Since $\frac{9}{10}$ is equivalent to $\frac{36}{40}$ and $\frac{7}{8}$ is equivalent to $\frac{35}{40}$, and 36 is greater than 35, $\frac{9}{10}$ is greater than $\frac{7}{8}$.

explicar Vocabulario académico Dar datos y detalles que hacen que una idea sea más fácil de comprender. Explicar puede incluir un resumen escrito apoyado por un diagrama, una gráfica, una tabla o una combinación de éstos.

términos relacionados: *analizar, aclarar, describir, justificar, decir*

ejemplo Explica por qué $\frac{9}{10}$ es mayor que $\frac{7}{8}$.

> Puedo escribir las fracciones en forma decimal y comparar los dígitos.
>
> | $\frac{9}{10}$ | 0.900 |
> |---|---|
> | $\frac{7}{8}$ | 0.875 |
>
> Puesto que 9 en el lugar de los décimos es mayor que 8, $\frac{9}{10}$ es mayor que $\frac{7}{8}$.
> También puedo escribir fracciones equivalentes con un común denominador y comparar los numeradores. Puesto que $\frac{9}{10}$ es equivalente a $\frac{36}{40}$ y $\frac{7}{8}$ es equivalente a $\frac{35}{40}$ y 36 es mayor que 35, $\frac{9}{10}$ es mayor que $\frac{7}{8}$.

F **fraction** A mathematical expression in the form $\frac{a}{b}$ where a and b are numbers. A fraction can indicate a part of a whole object or set, a ratio of two quantities, or a division. For the picture below, the fraction $\frac{3}{4}$ shows the part of the rectangle that is shaded. The denominator 4 indicates the number of equal-size pieces. The numerator 3 indicates the number of pieces that are shaded.

fracción Una expresión matemática que se expresa de esta forma: $\frac{a}{b}$ en la que a y b son números. Una fracción puede indicar una parte de un objeto o de un conjunto de objetos, una razón entre dos cantidades o una división. En el dibujo siguiente, la fracción $\frac{3}{4}$ muestra la parte del rectángulo que está coloreada. El denominador 4 indica la cantidad de piezas de igual tamaño. El numerador 3 indica la cantidad de piezas que están coloreadas.

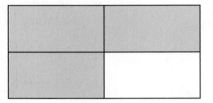

The fraction $\frac{3}{4}$ could also represent three of a group of four items meeting a particular criteria. For example, when 12 students enjoyed a particular activity and 16 students did not (the ratio is 3 to 4). Or, the amount of pizza each person receives when three pizzas are shared equally among four people ($3 \div 4$ or $\frac{3}{4}$ of a pizza per person).

La fracción $\frac{3}{4}$ también puede representar tres dentro de un grupo de cuatro objetos que cumplan con un mismo criterio. Por ejemplo, cuando 12 estudiantes participaron en una determinada actividad y 16 estudiantes no lo hicieron, (la razón es de 3 a 4), o la cantidad de pizza que le toca a cada persona cuando se reparten tres pizzas en partes iguales entre cuatro personas ($3 \div 4$ ó $\frac{3}{4}$ de pizza por persona).

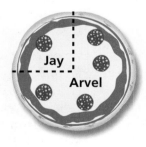

I **improper fraction** A fraction in which the absolute value of the numerator is greater than the absolute value of the denominator. The fraction $\frac{5}{2}$ is an improper fraction. The fraction $\frac{5}{2}$ means 5 halves and is equivalent to $2\frac{1}{2}$.

fracción impropia Una fracción cuyo el valor absoluto de numerador es mayor que el valor absoluto de denominador. La fracción $\frac{5}{2}$ es una fracción impropia. La fracción $\frac{5}{2}$ representa 5 mitades y equivale a $2\frac{1}{2}$.

M **mixed number** A number that is written with both a whole number and a fraction. A mixed number is the sum of the whole number and the fraction. The number $2\frac{1}{2}$ represents 2 wholes and a $\frac{1}{2}$ and can be thought of as $2 + \frac{1}{2}$.

número mixto Un número que se escribe con un número entero y una fracción. Un número mixto es la suma del número entero y la fracción. El número $2\frac{1}{2}$ representa 2 enteros y un $\frac{1}{2}$, y se puede considerar como $2 + \frac{1}{2}$.

N **numerator** The number written above the line in a fraction. In the fraction $\frac{5}{8}$, 5 is the numerator. When you interpret the fraction $\frac{5}{8}$ as a part of a whole, the numerator 5 tells that the fraction refers to 5 of the 8 equal parts.

numerador El número que se escribe sobre la barra en una fracción. En la fracción $\frac{5}{8}$, 5 es el numerador. Cuando se interpreta la fracción $\frac{5}{8}$ como parte de un entero, el numerador 5 indica que la fracción se refiere a 5 de 8 partes iguales.

O **opposites** Two numbers whose sum is 0. For example, −3 and 3 are opposites. On a number line, opposites are the same distance from 0 but in different directions from 0. The number 0 is its own opposite.

opuestos Dos números cuya suma da 0. Por ejemplo, −3 y 3 son opuestos. En una recta numérica, los opuestos se encuentran a la misma distancia del 0 pero en direcciones opuestas del 0 en la recta numérica. El número 0 es su propio opuesto.

P **percent** "Out of 100." A percent is a fraction in which the denominator is 100. When we write 68%, we mean 68 out of 100, $\frac{68}{100}$, or 0.68. We write the percent sign (%) after a number to indicate percent. The shaded part of this square is 68%.

porcentaje "De 100". Un porcentaje es una fracción en la que el denominador es 100. Cuando escribimos 68%, queremos decir 68 de 100, $\frac{68}{100}$ ó 0.68. Para indicar un porcentaje, escribimos el signo correspondiente (%) después del número. La parte coloreada de este cuadrado es el 68%.

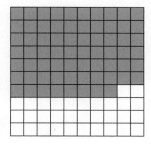

R **rate table** A table that shows the value of a single item in terms of another item. It is used to show equivalent ratios of the two items.

Movie Tickets

Number of people	1	2	3	4	5
Total Price	$12	$24	$36	$48	$60

tabla de tasas Una tabla que muestra el valor de un elemento con relación a otro elemento. Se usa para mostrar razones equivalentes de los dos elementos.

Boletos para el cine

Número de personas	1	2	3	4	5
Precio total	$12	$24	$36	$48	$60

ratio A comparison of two quantities expressed with a phrase such as 'the ratio of 3 to 5' which means '3 for every 5.' Such ratio comparisons are often written as common fractions and in the special notation 3 : 5.

$$\frac{3}{5} \qquad 3 \text{ to } 5 \qquad 3 : 5$$

razón Una comparación de dos cantidades que se expresa con frases como "la razón de 3 a 5", que significa "3 de cada 5". Con frecuencia, estas comparaciones se escriben como fracciones comunes $\frac{3}{5}$ y con la notación especial 3 : 5.

$$\frac{3}{5} \qquad 3 \text{ a } 5 \qquad 3 : 5$$

rational number Any number that can be written as the quotient of an integer and a non-zero integer, such as $\frac{3}{4}$, $\frac{13}{4}$, $\frac{3}{1}$, or $-\frac{3}{4}$.

número racional Cualquier número que se puede escribir como el cociente de un entero y de un entero distinto de cero, tales como $\frac{3}{4}$, $\frac{13}{4}$, $\frac{3}{1}$, ó $-\frac{3}{4}$.

T **tape diagram** A drawing that looks like a piece of tape, used to model expressions. Also called a bar model.

diagrama con tiras Un dibujo que parece una cinta y que se usa para representar expresiones matemáticas. También se llama modelo de barras.

U **unit fraction** A fraction with a numerator of 1. For example, in the unit fraction $\frac{1}{13}$, the part-whole interpretation of fractions tells us that 13 indicates the number of equal-size parts into which the whole has been split and that the fraction represents the quantity of 1 of those parts.

fracción unitaria Una fracción con numerador 1. Por ejemplo, en la fracción unitaria $\frac{1}{13}$, la interpretación de partes y enteros de fracciones nos dice que el 13 indica la cantidad de partes de igual tamaño en las que se divide el entero, y que la fracción representa la cantidad de una de esas partes.

unit rate A unit rate is a rate in which the second number (usually written as the denominator) is 1, or 1 of a quantity. For example, 1.9 children per family, 32 miles per gallon, and $\frac{3 \text{ flavors of ice cream}}{1 \text{ banana split}}$ are unit rates. Unit rates are often found by scaling other rates.

tasa por unidad Una comparación de dos cantidades mediante la división en la que el valor de la segunda cantidad, el divisor, es 1, ó 1 de una cantidad. Por ejemplo, 1.9 niños por familia, 32 millas por galón, y $\frac{3 \text{ sabores de helado}}{1 \text{ banana split}}$ son tasas por unidad. Las tasas por unidad se calculan a menudo poniendo a escala otras tasas.

Index

absolute value, 61, 64, 65, 85, 94

ACE
  connecting ratios and rates, 50–58
  making comparisons, 27–40
  number lines, 82–92
  percentages, 103–109

answers, explaining. *See* Mathematical Practices; Mathematical Reflections; reasoning, explaining your

base ten numeration, 71

benchmarks
  decimals and fractions, 80
  fractions and, 67–69, 78, 86
  percentages and, 107
  percent bars, 98

charts and graphs. *See also* fraction strips
  equivalent fractions and, 14
  fractions and, 31, 33
  grid models, 62, 71–72, 75, 88
  making comparisons, 12, 35, 37
  measuring progress, 21, 22, 24
  percentages and, 96
  percent bars, 97–98, 103
  place value charts, 74–75
  rate tables, 48–49, 52, 53–54, 100

common factors, 36

comparisons, making
  ACE, 27–40
  equivalent fractions, 14–19
  Mathematical Reflections, 41–42
  measuring progress, 20–22
  percentages and, 96, 101–102
  ratios and, 12–13, 101–102

using fractions and ratios, 9–11, 23–26
  world records, 7–9

comparison statements, 23, 26, 41

decimals
  benchmarks and, 107
  Explain Your Reasoning, 114
  fractions and, 79–81, 87, 88–90
  measurement and, 3
  number lines and, 74–78, 79–81
  percentages and, 95–96
  tenths and hundredths, 70–74

denominators, 38, 62, 71, 92, 95–96

differences, 2

equivalent decimals, 76, 77

equivalent fractions, 14–19, 28, 30, 41

equivalent ratios, 48

estimation
  estimating and ordering rational numbers, 67–69
  fractions and, 92
  percentages and, 96, 97–98, 100, 102, 103, 104

exchange rates, 58

Explain Your Reasoning, 114

factors, 34, 35, 36

"for every" claims, 37
  connecting ratios and rates, 43
  making comparisons, 10, 20, 23, 27, 29

fractions
  benchmarks and, 67–69, 86, 107

decimals and, 79–81, 88–90
  equivalent decimals and, 76, 77, 87
  Explain Your Reasoning, 114
  making comparisons, 9–11, 23–26
  Mathematical Reflections, 41
  measurement and, 3, 31–32
  number lines and, 79–81, 82
  numerators and denominators, 38
  percentages and, 95–96, 103, 104
  ratios and rates, 56, 57
  unit rates and, 44–45

fraction strips, 15, 16, 17–18
  decimals and, 76
  explaining your reasoning, 42
  measuring progress and, 20, 22
  number lines and, 28–29, 30
  ratios and, 27
  tenths and hundredths, 71

fundraising, making comparisons and, 7–26

genetic traits, 99–100

Glossary, 115–123

graphs. *See* charts and graphs

grid models, 62, 71–72, 75, 88

Guinness Book of World Records, 7–9

hieroglyphics, 19

hundredths, 95–96. *See also* tenths and hundredths

improper fractions, 61, 62, 65, 82–83

inequality statements, 83

integers and mixed numbers, 62–66

Index

Acknowledgments

Cover Design

Three Communication Design, Chicago

Photographs

Photo locators denoted as follows: Top (T), Center (C), Bottom (B), Left (L), Right (R), Background (Bkgd)

002 Kid Stock/Blend Images/Alamy; **003** Monkey Business Images/Shutterstock; **007** TWPhoto/Corbis; **008** Manchester Evening News; **043** Tom Stewart/Bridge/Corbis; **058** Ilya Genkin/Fotolia; **070** (TL) Exactostock/SuperStock, (C) Tetra Images/Alamy, (CL) Ed Zurga/Contributor/Getty Images, (TCR) Mbbirdy/E+/Getty Images, (BCR) only4denn/Fotolia; **079** Ullstein-CARO/Trappe/Glow Images; **099** (CL) Aaron Haupt/Photoresearchers, (TCL) Inti St Clair/Blend Images/Alamy, (TCR) Michael Newman/PhotoEdit,(CR) Custom Medical Stock Photo/Alamy, (BL) RedChopsticks Batch 19/Glow Asia RF/Alamy, (BCL) Kid Stock/Blend Images/Alamy,(BCR) Tatjana Romanova/Shutterstock, (CR) Piotr Marcinski/Fotolia; **104** Juniors Bildarchiv GmbH/Alamy; **106** Pearson Education.